THE ICING
ON THE CAKE!

Independence & Confidence

How to help your child achieve
the ultimate goal

Published in 2014 by Old Trees Press
(Melbourne, Australia)
PO Box 1008
Camberwell, Victoria, 3124, Australia
enquiry@OldTreesPress.com

Cover design and illustration: Mirela Tufan, www.mirela-tufan.com.au

National Library of Australia Cataloguing-in-Publication entry:

Author: Nicholson, Greg (Gregory Steven), 1954- author.

Title: The icing on the cake! : independence & confidence : how to
help your child achieve the ultimate goal / Greg Nicholson.

ISBN: 9780987210487 (paperback)

Subjects: Readiness for school.
Child development.
Early childhood education--Parent participation.
Self-confidence in children.

Dewey Number: 649.68

THE ICING ON THE CAKE!

Independence & Confidence

How to help your child achieve
the ultimate goal

Greg Nicholson

A psychologist's handbook for parents
preparing their youngsters for school

OLD TREES ✧ Melbourne

Early parenthood is a demanding, eventful time, throwing up more than a curved ball or two as we grapple with the rapid growth of our young children. As a new mother and busy clinical psychologist, I knew the instant I opened 'The ICing on the cake!' I had found the help I was seeking—practical, friendly advice that would not only reduce the trial-and-error frustrations of my daughter's preschool development, but importantly, bring out the best in our relationship.

Relaxed and good-humoured, and based on his experience as a psychologist and former infant teacher, author, Greg Nicholson, offers his easy-to-follow guidelines, enhancing his message with compelling anecdotes.

The author delivers on his front cover promise. The independence and confidence little ones need to carry them through their first year of school can begin at an early age by encouraging them to make small everyday decisions, says Nicholson—and don't forget the fun! Like stacking building blocks, accepting the topples when mistakes are made, young children gradually develop their skills and with them, the courage to experiment and try new challenges—an essential prerequisite to future learning.

I urge all parents of preschoolers to read this book. There is something in it for everyone—even a surprise or two for those who think there's nothing new to learn.

Sacha Serville, Clinical Psychologist

Contents

There were several titles suggested for this book, 'Have you done enough?', 'Easy as 1-2-3', 'Where do I start?', and so on, results of a typical editorial brainstorming session. As you will note, ultimately, *'The ICing on the cake'* prevailed—and did so for good reason: it distils the facets of learning contained in the following pages into a readily-grasped message.

In scanning the book's advice it will soon become clear that for kids, learning new skills in time for school—from coping with tricky shirt buttons and toilet rules, to the stuff of reciting home details and coming to grips with pencil holds—it all boils down to two crowning goals. These goals are:

▶ to step out onto the path of *independence,* and
▶ to develop self-*confidence*

But which comes first? Placed on a circle, you will see that each nourishes and complements the other: confidence builds independence—and independence builds confidence. Whichever may take the lead, when any successful learning meets the finish line, together they take a bow and move on to the next challenge.

Your child's journey will mean the excitement of making new friends, testing new experiences and coming to understand that falling down and getting up again is the fast track to learning both at home and at school.

In embracing the ultimate goal—*the icing on the cake*—you will be giving your preschooler the very best opportunity to become not only an accomplished student, but a well-adjusted, self-assured adult equipped for the coming times.

I would be delighted to hear from you should you have a question pertaining to your child's progress as you test the guidelines. My contact details are at the end of the book, page 239.

In the meantime, I wish you and your family every success and a very happy life together.

Greg Nicholson, 2014

By the very nature of written English conventions in the West, modern global authors must face issues of grammar and spelling differences as they seek to maintain acceptable universal texts. I am acutely conscious of this in my role as an educator. Therefore, to American moms and dads, I'm signalling a caveat that the odd word or two and some conventions in this book differ marginally from US English.

With cap still in hand, apologies, too, to parents of little girls. To overcome the inherent difficulty of covering 'him' and 'her' child genders, and for reading efficiency, my editor suggested I use the male term to represent both. Frankly, I favoured the female gender, so we tossed a coin. My editor won. You have my permission, therefore, to blame her for any misgivings.

Finally, the text indicates this book is 'for parents'. I use the term loosely. If you permanently care for a child—be you married, single, divorced or separated, straight, gay, a grandparent or other guardian—it is no less written for you. If I've overlooked you, I stand corrected. Feel free to jump in. If you are among that assorted mix of heroic humans who love and look after kids, this book is definitely for you.

Occupational therapy

If you have concerns that your child is experiencing slowness or greater difficulty than you believe is normal for his age in performing activities which involve the body's motor skills—the small and large muscle groups used, for example, in dressing, writing and at play—I suggest, through your family doctor, you contact a qualified children's occupational therapist in your area who may offer advice, and therapy should it be needed.

Room 1, day one of infant school intake. Parents, mostly mothers, pressed through the door of my classroom, clutching the hands of their children or ushering them ahead, shoulder to shoulder in the squeeze. The usual expressions were all there: a mix of joy and trepidation on parents and kids alike. On the faces of the children, bright ready grins and secret glances told me, *I am grown up now,* while faint little smiles said they weren't quite sure.

Amid the jostle, a young father caught my eye and nodded quickly, his hand on the shoulder of his son. He looked uneasy, out of his comfort zone. His son stared straight ahead, pale and wide-eyed. As the boy held back, the father bent to his ear and motioned towards me with his chin. The child looked across the room, regarded me with a trembling lip and burst into tears. Whatever his anxious dad had said, it hadn't paid off. I was instantly reminded how easily parental emotions can be sensed and transferred to a child.

Cheerfully, I waved the father in and amid the introductions, engaged them both with some friendly chat to ease the small lad's fears.

With parents and children now milling around me, I felt a bump at my hip. A hand was thrust up holding a coloured-in drawing torn from a colouring book. 'Mr. Nicholson, Mr. Nicholson,' a happy voice chirped, 'I coloured this for you!' Another child, eager-faced and prompted by her beaming, pink-cheeked mother, held up her gift to be admired.

I accepted the offering with a smile and a word and looked about. The morning was presenting no surprises. Just another perfectly normal first day of school—a lovely mix of excited new kids: some confident, some shy, some happy, some scared out of their wits.

I am sure many of us recall our own moments at the edge of that Rubicon—the confronting of our first teacher—at the beginning of a scholastic journey that would shape who and what we were to become.

Being that first teacher to many, I had always felt a sense of privilege to be charged with guiding those young minds in their very first steps along the formal learning path. At the same time, I felt a heavy responsibility: it was my aim during that first important year, to not only instil self-confidence in my students but, above all, to lay the foundations that would inspire their love of learning. And in the first week of intake, I knew intuitively which ones would need most help and which would rise quickly to the top as the class slipped tellingly into two groups: those who had been prepared for school before reaching the school gates—and those who had not.

B efore her fledglings are grown, a mother bird will guard them with her life. But comes the day she knows they are ready, she calls them from the nest and the training begins—her spur: the instinct for survival. It's a bird-eat-bird, cat-eat-bird, predatory world and, in their daily search for food, unless they learn to fend for themselves, her young will not live to see summer.

Fortunately, our challenges are not as grim. Even so, the quality of our home environment and the training we experience from our parents or guardians *before* we step out for school are held by many researchers to be as significant as school itself in setting the course of our passage through childhood.

As a parent of a preschooler, you may therefore be asking yourself, *'Am I doing it right?* Am I doing enough? Will my child's school journey be a reasonably smooth run—or are we in for a bumpy ride?'

In the coming pages, I hope to ease your concerns. I will also show you how you can offer your son or daughter the very brightest opportunity for a confident start to school—one that can be recalled with fondness and gratitude in the years to come.

Life's important building blocks

Recently, I read US research which identified distinct psychological differences between well-behaved and not-so-well behaved athletes.

Forensic psychologist, Jeffrey Pfeifer, found that in a study of sixty elite sportspeople, those with histories of crime had experienced little decision-making in their earlier lives. Such subjects were found to lack empathy and self-control, were overly self-centred and believed they would never be caught out behaving badly.

The study supports advice I have been giving young parents in my role as a psychologist and educator for more than two decades: if you value a positive outcome for your child's future development, begin *early* to involve your young one in the natural process of decision-making. No need to be heavy. Just easy, everyday choices—and don't forget the fun:

▸ Should we cut our bread with a fork or a . . . ?
▸ Would you like half a glass of milk, or a full glass?
▸ Shall we take our puppy on our walk?

Allowing children to make simple choices on a daily basis, importantly, teaches them to be discerning, and fosters their first small steps towards independence. This means that without fanfare, youngsters begin to assemble essential building blocks of life—increasing their chances of a happy, stable childhood and of becoming confident, thinking adults.

At your next opportunity when there are no likely distractions, I would suggest before we begin, you indulge in some quiet introspection.

At the end of this topic, stop reading and sit back for a moment or two, eyes closed, and think about the primary focus of this book—your child—and all that he means to you. Picture him: his physical appearance, his little idiosyncrasies and all the things about him that make you smile and want to hug him.

Then, take a journey through time. He is emerging from his last day at school or college at the age of eighteen. What does he look like? Who is he as he boards a bus for home or slings his books into the back seat of your car? Have your expectations been realised? What has your teenager achieved academically, and what nature of person has he become?

As you reflect on this future setting, be aware that the world has advanced by some fourteen or fifteen years. This means in the time-frame presented you are living in the 2020s, and no one can predict with any certainty what key issues will be dominating your community, national forums or the global stage.

What is a surety, however, is that the world is very different, imposing vast challenges upon its leaders, new expectations and demands on its workforces and affecting employers and their staff at individual levels.

In this imagined era, interdependent disciplines and issues spread to, and impact, even the smallest corners of the world: the efficiency of our energy delivery, the sustainability of community development, unpredictable weather patterns and climate change, responsible policy-making, health management issues related to new and robust diseases, endeavours in the realm of peaceful solutions to conflict, and the significance of collaboration, problem solving, scientific advances and invention in all fields.

Complex, isn't it? These are not the halcyon days of the 1950s you may have read or heard about. This 2020s decade is exciting, yes. But the challenges are bigger, broader, more convoluted, more intricate and harder to manage and solve than any decades before in recent modern times—and it will affect everyone.

Will your child be ready for this world, fourteen or fifteen years from now? Will he be poised to become a productive member of society connected to the world at large? Will he be equipped to fulfil his potential as an adult? What has he taken from the school journey that brought him to this important threshold? And are you satisfied that at this point in his development, he is all you had hoped he would be, possessing qualities and skills that will carry him through the first phase of his adult life?

You cannot know, of course.

But let us return to the reality of the here and now and the purpose of this book: to help you prepare your youngster for a smooth transition to school. For that is what it can be; what it should be—an exciting and happy beginning—one which will allow him to build confidence and resilience, and to enhance his potential for learning life skills.

This is where his future begins.

Your preschooler's physical world

Hands, feet and . . . whoops-a-daisy!

Remember when your baby first pulled himself up on very wobbly legs, his face shining, as he gripped the rail? And later, as he took his first steps, he teetered on the brink, plonked down on his bottom and immediately raised himself up to try again.

Your little one was making his very first bid for independence.

Not only was he physically engaging with the world around him, he was learning through his instincts, life's early lessons: what didn't work (his mistake), how to get it right (his solution), and that practice created the desired outcome (his skill).

Remember the excitement of that first step? His delight? He was so proud of himself! You probably made a fuss and praised him for being clever—and in the next year or so in your tender care, he continued to learn and grow.

So now that he is three or four, with the first year of school looming on the horizon, you naturally want to continue building his independence to prepare him for, arguably, the most important phase of his life.

That you are reading this, is evidence of your smart intentions. But at the same time as a young parent, you may be wondering with life so busy, whether you will always keep your eye on the ball. Fear not! This handbook will help you tick all the boxes well ahead of schedule, and hopefully prove a useful companion.

Before we continue, a couple of pointers are critical:

A red light should be flashing at this word.

Anxious though you may be for your child's welfare, remember that mollycoddling *does not* encourage independence. It smothers it! So give your preschooler room to breathe and stretch, to test things out and grow. And that means in preparing him as presented here for all that lies ahead, relax, but remain supportive and patient. *Allow him to fail.* Remind yourself of a simple irony: 'falling down' is another building block of life—a step towards achievement— and often (indeed, usually) a key part of learning.

See more in our chapter on over-protective parenting, page 155.

Another important point:

When your child gets things right, *praise him*. Be sure to give due weight to his *effort in mastering the skill*—'Good boy for trying so hard. You did it! I am so proud of you,' and so on.

Nurturing his sense of self-belief through praise for achievement during his early learning journey will see independence and confidence blossom hand in hand.

Praise and its effects will be discussed in a moment, including an aspect of praise you may not be aware of that could have the opposite result that you intend on your child. Although an intangible factor in a child's physical world, when employed correctly, praise proves a key motivator as he continues to explore and test his emerging capabilities. An understanding of how it works, before we set off, will therefore be useful.

But let's dive into a box of skills we can call, 'Playing *school* before you go', to see what is needed.

Grab a coffee if you like, and we'll get started.

In preparing for school, the development of certain skills are easier than others and the time it takes to learn them varies with each child. To ensure a relaxed environment and allowing for different learning rates, I suggest you begin your child's training *no less than* six months before the big day—but longer is better.

Youngsters *love* to play 'school'. This can provide a number of positive learning activities under one entertaining umbrella: dressing, lunch box meals, themes that develop body motor skills, and so on. Approached without censure in a relaxed manner, playing school—often initiated by kids themselves—can prompt lively expectations that they're not only about to enjoy a game, but to cross the threshold of the enthralling new world of being grown-up boys and girls.

Commencing from the comfort zone of a regular playtime routine, your conversation might go something like: 'Let's play . . . *school!* What shall we do today? What about . . . getting *dressed* for school? Okay. Now where are those special clothes? Here they are, right here in your drawer!' And so on.

So—let's begin with our topic on praise then we'll go on to the dressing game.

Praise—beware! A two-sided coin

Over the years, countless parents have come to me, starry-eyed, to tell me how smart or intelligent their child was. Yes, some were bright, one or two even highly gifted, but truth to tell, the majority struggled to live up to the labels their doting parents had imposed on them since they had walked at ten months, or reeled off the alphabet from the age of three.

One such little boy was Alexander who was thrust through my Prep classroom door one year, *the day before* the first day of school as I was organising desks and learning aids. He was followed by his mother and two smiling grandparents who all proceeded to tell me as the boy looked on, how advanced he was for his years, and to ask what they could expect that would ensure the blossoming and growth of his special gifts. As evidence of his 'special gifts', Alexander was then encouraged by his mother to recite the capital cities of various countries of the world, which he parroted with admirable ease.

In view of his entourage, I gained the impression that young Alex, an only child who could do no wrong, was the apple not only of his mother's eye but also those of his grandparents. I wondered, having already been down a similar path with other families, how the coming term would unfold. As it happened, I didn't have to wait beyond the first day to find out.

The kids were enjoying a lively exchange in class on what they'd done over the public holidays and I noted that Alexander, who'd been raised at home to believe he was a very clever boy, was one of the quieter ones; his mouth was closed tight as a clam and when I glanced at him, he quickly dropped his eyes.

Later in the week, during developmental role playing in small groups, he sat on a chair and watched as the other children pretended to be market stall holders and customers selling and buying produce. Had I not intervened, I believe Alex would have continued to lay low hoping not to be noticed, minimising his presence in class and becoming increasingly less engaged with classroom activities and learning.

The year before Alexander, I'd taught another child whom the kids had affectionately dubbed, 'Bozie', described glowingly by his parents as 'very bright' but who, instead of performing well, transformed himself into the classroom clown to mask his anxiety over a need to live up to his 'smart' tag by getting all his answers right.

I used a similar strategy to manage both situations.

Although their secondary behaviour had manifested in different ways, the underlying issue was that each child had been afraid to take risks for fear of failing— for fear of being embarrassed or thought of as 'dumb' when confronted with new learning on unfamiliar ground. Their parents had done the boys no favours.

Unwittingly leading them to believe they were so smart they could wing any topic—that with natural ability they didn't have to think or put in any effort was, and is—even for the majority—*just not so.*

Learning is multifaceted, demanding far more than a quick intellect. Drawing on our environment for information, it takes curiosity, character and our vast pool of mental resources to achieve its end. Without persistence and resilience, the walls of challenge can readily block our path and, without *confidence*, there is barely a breath of wind to lift our wings.

To redress the issue and encourage Bozie and the following year, Alexander, to find their classroom confidence—during discussions and simple problem solving I ignored the quick-answer kids and gently asked the quieter children in a non-judgmental way what *they* thought, giving positive acknowledgement of their responses in front of the class. When I then asked Alexander to be a class monitor for the week, and later, because he was 'being so responsible', if he could teach his successor, Rachel, what to do, it was as if a different child had walked into the room.

Both Alex and Bozie opened like flowers in bloom. In a rush of self-belief, they began to join in spiritedly to our discussions and became eagerly engaged in story writing and other class activities. No longer having to hide behind masks of disinterest—as had Alexander— or zany disruptive behaviour—as had Bozie—both boys became active classroom participants.

If you've guessed by now from this discussion on praise that all praise is not equal, you're right. *Praise is a two-sided coin.*

Praise for effort has the power to motivate and *build* confidence in a child, while words that praise for intelligence alone, although well intended, have the potential to *undermine* or even destroy confidence; it can deliver a heavy burden and produce, as I found in my classroom, undesirable behaviour.

Memories of Alexander and Bozie came back to me recently when I read of studies by Dr Carol Dweck, a social psychology professor at Stanford University.

Older research had suggested praising a child for being smart or intelligent buoyed their confidence. Questioning this widely-held view, however, Dweck, a scholar of motivation, intelligence theories and childhood learning over four decades, tested 400 fifth-graders and found a quite different and disquieting story: she and her team identified two mindsets in the students about their own abilities which ran counter to one another, and showed the impact of those mindsets on student motivation.

Analysing the fifth-graders' responses during a series of easy and hard tests over several days, the two opposed mindsets were what Dweck calls a *fixed* mindset and a *growth* mindset.

Kids with fixed mindsets tend to think, for example, that their ability is something they're born with; that their talents are a fixed trait—that they're an inherent, unchangeable feature of who they are.

Dweck observed that fixed mindset students believe they have a certain amount of intelligence and that's that. 'Then,' she said, 'their goal becomes to look smart all the time and never look dumb.'

Students exhibiting a growth mindset, on the other hand, believe their talents and skills can be learned— that they can be developed through effort and good teaching. 'They don't necessarily think everyone's the same or anyone can be Einstein, but they believe everyone can get smarter if they work at it,' said Dweck, who repeated her experiments with similar results.

Professor Dweck noted that although her extensive research has involved older children whose maturity allows their articulation of feelings and beliefs, such mindsets have also been identified in *preschoolers of three or four years of age.* (My emphasis.)

Dweck's fifth-grader study started with a non-verbal intelligence quotient (IQ) test comprising a series of easy puzzles, where most kids performed well. Delivering the marks individually outside the classroom, the researchers—randomly dividing the students into groups—offered three different sets of praise:

- *praise for intelligence:* 'Wow, you got eight right; that's a really good score. You must be smart at this!' (Experimental group)
- *praise for effort:* 'Wow, you got eight right; that's a really good score. You must have tried really hard.' (Experimental group)
- *praise for results:* 'Wow, that's a really good score.' (Control group)

The follow-up revealed dramatic results, identifying the different mindsets: the kids were asked what puzzles they'd like to work on next. They were told they could select easy tasks, or ones posing challenge and likely mistakes, but that great things could be learned through attempting them.

Most of the students praised for being smart chose—the easy puzzles! During a talk at Stanford, Dweck commented, the kids weren't fools. 'They wanted to keep on looking smart,' she said. 'They wanted to keep that label.'

The majority of youngsters praised for effort, however, rose avidly to the challenge and became engaged in the tasks. They were *motivated to learn*, in spite of being told they'd probably make errors. Some even said later that the hardest tasks were their favourites.

Being confronted by tests or conditions that could produce failure or embarrassment in front of others can have a numbing or otherwise negative effect on children with a fixed mindset. We saw the reactions of Alexander and Bozie, raised on a pedestal by their parents for their 'giftedness': they tried to dodge under the radar or clowned around to cover their fears.

When Dweck's fifth-graders were given yet another test—one beyond their years, at which, as the research team predicted, *all the kids failed*—the fixed mindset students, having rejected the significance of effort, believing their innate ability was their only resource, fell into a heap. Without a perceived framework for dealing with failure, they simply had nowhere to turn.

These kids believed they'd failed because they weren't smart after all. Critically, this undermined their confidence and motivation to the extent that Dweck's final task—designed to be as easy as the first—sent their scores plummeting by some twenty per cent, compared to the start.

Meanwhile, the growth mindset youngsters had their hands firmly on the controls and motivation was high. They believed that exercising some mental muscle would throw up solutions, even if it meant a temporary setback or two along the way.

Learning and skill-building are of course about effort. But they're also as much about getting something *wrong* as getting it right. I said recently to a Year 7 tuition student who was stressing over a routine problem solving exercise: 'Slow down, take a breath and see the problem for what it is: it's a great opportunity to refine your skills. So, test an idea! If it doesn't work, guess what? *You've learned something!* When you then try a premise that does work, guess what again? *You've learned something else* and can move on.'

That's what Dweck's growth mindset fifth-graders did. In their last easy task—in which the fixed mindset kids had fared worse by some twenty per cent—this group of young risk-takers showed a thirty per cent increase on their first test scores.

When I show my students—kids of all ages across a broad demographic, seeking to sharpen their academic skills—that they can step beyond their innate ability to *make* their own success, many have an 'aha!' moment.

Learning *how to learn* and to think for themselves is exciting and empowering! The light suddenly dawns that by concentrating and working at it, *they* can be a force to help shape their own outcomes.

But what about *teaching* a growth mindset? In her scientific endeavours on learning, motivation and the diverse effects of praise, Carol Dweck explored this, too: whether students' poor academic performances could be enhanced through learning about intelligence. Again, her results were impressive.

In her study, 100 underperforming 7th graders were randomly divided into two groups. Group A (the controls) were tutored over several sessions on study skills only. Group B (the test group) received study skills, but also two sessions on how the brain works.

The Group Bs were captivated! They read an essay that told them they could *grow* their intelligence: 'New research shows the brain can be developed like a muscle,' said the essay. When the brain gets a work out, the Group Bs learned, it forms new nerve cells and, over time, gets stronger—gets smarter.

'This riveted the students,' said Dweck. 'They loved learning about the brain! They'd never thought about it, how it worked . . . that what they did had a direct impact on their brain and the connections it made.'

These students later markedly improved their maths results. But the Group As, who'd learned nothing on the wonders of the brain—how effort could make them smarter—lacked the inspiration to apply their new study skills, and continued to under-perform.

Professor Dweck's research is a gift to the complex world of raising children. Most of us have probably told our kids—particularly in their early learning phases—how 'clever' or 'smart' they were to learn even a small step of a new skill. It's natural; you've probably done it; I know I have, and no harm done—my kids have grown into confident, resilient young people.

The message, however, is in the detail. It's about balance; about the words we use, about moderation, our manner and being alert to the fact that little ones will take what we tell them at face value. If we say, 'You're so clever! You're the smartest kid I know,' a four-year-old will puff up and believe he's king of the castle. Say it too often and we must ask ourselves whether a child is at risk of forming an over-inflated sense of his intelligence—of developing a fixed mind-set—and all that it implies.

There is much more to be learned from this interesting topic that is beyond the scope of this book; you may wish to explore further. Notes for Professor Dweck's work are at the end of the chapter to assist you, while below, is a handful of children's titles you may wish to share with your child, highlighting achievement through effort, perseverance, positive thinking and self-belief. Find them on Amazon.com.

> ▸ *The Little Engine That Could* by Watty Piper
> ▸ *Green Eggs and Ham* by Dr. Seuss
> ▸ *Long Shot: Never Too Small to Dream Big* by Chris Paul and Frank Morrison
> ▸ *The Very Clumsy Click Beetle* by Eric Carl

In summarising—a last word. If in the past you've sought to inspire your preschooler or older child, by perhaps telling him he's the smartest kid on the block, save a thought for Alexander and Bozie. At four, Alex could perfectly parrot the capitals of the world, yet had no understanding of what or where Washington, DC, was and no concept of London or Beijing or Paris or Rome—to him, they were just a bunch of new words. Bozie, for his part, could do brilliant headstands and walk on his hands. Neither child was gifted! Yet both had been led to believe they were so bright, life would be a cakewalk—that was, until they faced the unsettling reality of the classroom.

So avoid misunderstandings. Think before you speak and don't smother your youngster with praise at every turn. Bestow it where it is truly due and steer clear of generalisations like, 'What a nice picture!' That is, make it more meaningful: you can heighten the impact and build greater confidence by pinpointing *a* particular part of a task or skill *to show you noticed.* 'I like the way you coloured in the lady's hat. Well done! It looks quite special.' Your child knows that he gave his all to that hat, and your recognition of the fact will find its mark. Just watch his face.

Remember the aim: your child's autonomy—the ability to achieve on his own. So don't rush in to help too soon. Step back and let him work things through. Challenge and frustration are a natural part of learning. When he masters a skill unaided, his instincts will tell him your words are deserved.

Actually, I'd venture to say, this business of praise may not be that complicated. If you forget, and make a blunder with, 'Wow, you're smart!'—relax. You can get out of jail fast with a swift escape clause:

'I'm impressed; you worked so hard at that, son!'

Notes

Dweck, C.S. 'Self-theories: Their motivation, personality and development.' *Psychology Press, Philadelphia,* 1999.

Dweck, C.S. 'Mindset: The new psychology of success.' *Random House, New York,* 2006.

VanDeVelde, C. 'Carol Dweck: Praising Intelligence: Costs to Children's Self-Esteem and Motivation.' *Bing Nursery School, Stanford University,* November, 2007.

Bronson, Po and Merryman, Ashley. 'Nurtureshock.' *Ebury Press, an imprint of Ebury Publishing, a Random House Group company,* 2009.

Dressing

If there is one thing that will accelerate a pre-schooler's independence, it's learning to dress himself. This achievement not only contributes to his self-belief and pride, but overcomes potential early difficulties at school, be it going to the toilet or changing shoes for sport.

Playing 'dress ups' and getting dressed and undressed in special clothes for school provide confidence as well as aiding development of fine motor skills. 'Going to school' games also present quiet moments—as you help with buttons, for example—to introduce positive school topics of what he can expect there—'just like kinder', if he attends kindergarten—such as a nice big playground, making more friends, singing new songs, painting pictures, and even writing with *pencils!*

Learning to dress and to undress at night, perhaps before a bath, can and should begin in simple form, well before the age of four. If it's time for getting dressed, begin by undertaking most of the task yourself but leaving one easy item for your child to complete: pulling up socks in the morning or pyjamas at night are good ways to start.

Gradually doing less yourself, allow your child to do more, remembering to praise him for each small accomplishment. Be thoughtful in your choice of clothing, ensuring buttonholes are not a struggle and that buttons can be readily slipped through.

If school arrives before shoe laces are mastered (this earns special mention, page 57), consider shoes with Velcro tabs, if fitting, until laces are no longer an issue.

Small fingers need plenty of practice.

As a new mother, my wife made a large stuffed 'training' doll, following a paper pattern. He had long dangly arms and legs, shoe laces sewn in place on the feet, and a cheerful smiling face. He was dressed in a brightly coloured shirt with fasteners at the front, and a pair of bibbed trousers with a zip. Big embroidered numbers on the trouser legs prompted the name, *'One-Two'*. One-Two's bib straps, featuring large red buttons, were buttoned and unbuttoned a thousand times across the early years of three children. Such was the love and value attached to this doll, he became a constant companion, dragged on overseas trips and earning special place of honour at the kids' birthday parties. A very subtle little teacher was One-Two!

If you are free to choose school clothes, easy wash and wear items will ease the domestic front—the washing machine will likely still get a good workout during your child's first school year: chalk, crayons, paints, sauce and mud—*whoohoo,* people!

Be patient with your child at this time. Yes, caring for one's clothes is part of the training, but should be viewed in context. He'll be taking on significant new challenges and will need time to adjust. So don't get cranky. Praise him for his achievements. Think of *his* day.

Walking in his small shoes will bring its rewards.

It is no accident that 'dressing' has led the charge of preparation skills. It is *too late* to tackle this once your child begins school. Among other reasons is the early morning rush: getting dressed with time to spare avoids anxiety and stress, and promotes a relaxed, convivial atmosphere. As a psychologist, among the many issues parents present is that of 'problem' children who refuse to dress on time. This often reflects issues of power and control within the family dynamics at the heart of which lies—not the children—but the parents who have failed to establish firm family rules and expectations.

Smart parents, take note! *Rewarding successful, independent behaviour at a child's early age goes a long way to avoiding such problems.*

So make your rules and guard them like a rock! If they are broken, stand by the consequences you have also put in place—withdrawing favourite activities like bedtime stories, perhaps, friends over to play or promised treats—for a day or so. And be aware that consequences are useless unless they cause a good dose of child disappointment and reflection.

But keep the scales even. Rules and consequences should be balanced by rewards for reaching goals—and *learning to dress* can be one of them; youngsters, especially, will love the kudos you bestow as they master every step, striving to achieve more, and to please you. The ultimate aim—dressing in good time—not only avoids conflict, but shows respect for others and should be a golden family rule.

The machinations of power

Ever watched a toddler scream blue murder in the supermarket? He may well be in pain—but chances are, when the mother finds a candy bar, the tantrum is turned off like a switch.

This is classic 'power and control' at work in the expert hands of an infant. We all feel for the mother as she reaches in panic for the quick fix. But truth to tell, she should be chastised for losing her authority to a two-year-old, simply through failing to teach appropriate behaviour at home.

Where were the boundaries—*the rules and expectations* imposed on her son—the protective barriers with consequences for their breach, within which the child was expected to stay? Governments call it *law and order*. We can call it, 'learning acceptable behaviour'.

Kids need boundaries to feel secure. And the first thing they'll do—like our toddler—is nudge them to test their strength. If structures give to pressure or are absent, children feel vulnerable, exposed. Rebellion can result—unwelcome, antisocial behaviour—that might be read as a silent appeal: 'Hey, I'm just learning this gig. So now I've misbehaved, tell me what to do!'

Unacceptable conduct fuelled by poor parenting can cause family conflict, triggering a domino effect. Worse, it can set a trend of wilful disobedience in childhood and later, parent-mirrored behaviour which not surprisingly can be passed to the next generation. You may have heard it said: 'He's *just* like his mother!'

Parents who are consistent and strong—but cool to be with—have a healthy chance of raising happy kids.

Activity

Put a fun chart on the fridge, featuring the different skills at each stage of dressing which can be ticked off when achieved. If your child has dressed himself, managing buttons or zips, for example, affix a large bright sticker against the skill and honour him with a small reward at the end of the week. Rewards are great motivators!

Undressing is much easier than dressing and is a good way to introduce the topic at an early age— at age one, most infants take great joy in pulling off their socks and by three or four, they should be identifying the front and back of clothes. As you approach the more complex aspects of dressing, aid your youngster by demonstrating that over-the-head items, such as T-shirts, for example, can be put on more readily if laid on a bed or chair, front facing down. Don't assume he will automatically know front from back. Show him that the front has the motif or similar, the back, a label, and choose clothes reflecting these features.

Having been shown, once he starts to manage any stage on his own under your watchful eye, step back and *allow him to sort it out himself.* Don't rush it! Offer encouragement and applause and help out only if it's absolutely necessary.

Those pesky shoe laces

If you avoid those pesky shoe-lace-tying rituals because they're difficult and time consuming and because Velcro tabs are a useful substitute, I understand, but advise against it. You will be denying your youngster a practical opportunity to develop the small muscles of his fingers essential for writing and which form a vital component of fine motor skills (page 77). Tying his own shoe laces will also mean bringing him one step closer to independence.

Another value of learning to tie shoe laces lies in the sequencing of steps: step one, step two, step three, and so on. Understanding the nature of sequences is fundamental to early schooling, and the more exposure a child has to such activities, the better.

I have watched five-year-olds successfully teach their classmates how to tie shoe laces. It takes practice, but if they can do it, so can you!

To prevent your child from being overwhelmed or frustrated, encourage him to complete *one* aspect only of tying his shoe laces and build upon each step, praising him as he masters every stage. *Start early and take your time.*

To tie laces 'bunny ears' style, a pictorial learning tool can be found at the Raising Children Network website at raisingchildren.net.au. Search for 'shoe laces' on its homepage.

Demonstrations on *YouTube* may also be of help. You and your child will work out which style works best, but one thing I have noticed is that few demonstrations offer the starting point of *right lace over left* to commence the tying process, which gives a *firm* straight bow across the shoe width. It's not rocket science, but here is my 'bow and arrow' method:

Activity

1. Start, as mentioned, with the right lace over left threaded under, and pull both laces tight.
2. Near the tie, using the left hand, curl the fingers around the left-hand-side lace and grip with the thumb, pressing down to hold the tie in place.
3. Point the left index finger across the shoe like an arrow over which to make a loop with the other lace using the right hand. Press the middle fingertip on the tie to hold it firmly.
4. Place the left-side lace over the loop, scooping it under with a left finger into the space near the fingertip hold. Keeping the pressure, pull both loops taut with fingertips and thumbs.
5. Voila! A firm straight bow across the shoe width.
6. Now, for the other shoe! Flat laces help little fingers to push the laces through the spaces.

Note: If you tie another knot on top—if the laces are too long and droopy, for example—don't make it tight; your child may have trouble untying it.

Going to the toilet

Your four-year-old is at a party. Or playing with a friend. Or simply with you at home, fixing Lego. Perhaps you're on a picnic in a park and there's a ball game in progress. Whatever the venue, the common theme is that your child is utterly enthralled. *Totally absorbed in the moment.* Suddenly, he finds your eyes across the grass or room, a sheepish look on his face: *Uh-oh! Sorry, Dad—I've just had a bit of an accident!*

On the rocky road to independence, such daytime wetting events are normal—a part of growing up.

Even so, a new era beckons. Whilst your child relies on your care for many of his young needs, just as when a toddler he grew out of nappies, as a preschooler soon to head off on his own, now he must learn to take full responsibility for his toilet routine—in other words, *to listen to, and respond to,* the signals of his own body.

But whoa, hold on. By age four, a kid's world has become more wondrous, more astonishing and breathtakingly exciting than ever. His fertile young brain is having more fun than a barrel of monkeys.

Jumping jellybeans! What a galaxy of glorious distractions there is to be had—so many marvellously magical, overwhelmingly awesome gadgets, gizmos and games to engage the mind. Does a four-year-old child, on the brink of discovering the world, *always* hear that faint inner voice tugging at his consciousness?

Of course not! All too late, his bladder is shouting, *Hey, did you hear me? I need to go NOW!*

You may have been lulled into believing that after successful nappy training you were home and dry. Your focus is on other matters. But so is your child's. With his eye off the ball—or *on* it in the park, as the case may well be—his inner senses training will sometimes take flight.

It's usually a minor mishap. You can be back on dry ground again pretty fast through repeated reminders to your youngster to 'listen to your body' *even when playing games.* And when going out, teach him to tell himself, 'I should go to the toilet before I leave.'

It is at such times that your child's good training in responding promptly, efficiently and step by step to the toileting process is all important: zips or buttons, tucking in clothes, flushing the toilet, wiping the seat if necessary, and thoroughly washing hands are key to teaching your youngster sound toilet management. (A few pointers for accident avoidance follow shortly.)

Normal events aside, if your child wets regularly during the day, or begins daytime wetting after four years of age, your family doctor can test for possible common bladder problems, including a urinary tract infection (UTI) which may require antibiotics.

That duly noted, some youngsters may have daytime wetting episodes due to stress, or may use wetting to seek your attention. More discussion on these issues follows the tips for avoiding accidents.

Avoiding accidents during training

- With a gold star chart and reward system firmly in place, consistently remind your child about them—and of the treasure in store for visiting the toilet in time, especially when going out.
- Before leaving the house, routinely visit the bathroom yourself to model the right behaviour, then ask your child to go also.
- There are bound to be accidents, nonetheless. When leaving home, be sure to pack 'wipes' and a change of clothing along with your keys.
- Wherever you are, at home or out, if your youngster is absorbed in a project or play, *physically remove him* from the area to gain his attention and ask if he needs to go to the toilet.
- Your child may not be fussed by wet pants, but be assured, others soon will be. If totally distracted having fun, he may simply shake his head at your questioning, regardless of whether or not he needs to go. Make it your mission to therefore take him to the bathroom at reasonably regular intervals.
- Don't delay when your child gives you the signal; in early training, especially, you won't have much time.
- If you're in a leafy setting, check where the toilets are as soon as you arrive—or when all else fails, locate the nearest bush.

A telling case at one school was recently reported in the media. The school required whole grades of kids to troop to the toilet together, causing a spike in children wetting themselves and suffering constipation. A comfortable stress-free state should clearly accompany toileting. Where there's no pressure, there's no anxiety.

If you suspect your child is daytime wetting to seek your attention, it's important that you do not criticise or show anger. Anger *is* 'giving your attention' and is counter-productive, as you might guess: *Wow, this wetting caper works; I should try this again. She's really taking notice of me now!*

Minimising your response to the negative conduct and rewarding positive outcomes with warm hugs and praise will greatly pay dividends. If attention-seeking wetting occurs, tell your child firmly his behaviour is unacceptable. Then go away and ignore him; do something else for fifteen minutes or so, and it will send a strong message: *Well that didn't work!* By next introducing the idea of a reward for good behaviour— perhaps as you chat while getting clean underwear— your child will be doing some smart calculations.

Observing the 'avoiding accidents' guidelines, if he wets but stays dry the next day, applaud his effort with a gold star, or award a 'well done' sticker as a Badge of Honour and let him swagger around the house for a bit; stationers will stock the stickers. Promise a reward for several dry days hence, and praise him mightily for being grown-up after each achievement day.

If there's another accident, be consistent and do not fuss: that is, be calm, supportive and understanding. Recall when he fell down as an infant attempting to walk and use a similar positive response: 'Whoops-a-daisy! Let's find some nice dry clothes, shall we?'

It behoves me, however, to ask the outstanding question and one you might ask yourself: If your child *is* seeking attention, why is this so? Upon honest self-assessment, if you believe there may be room for improvement in your relationship with your child and that you could rearrange your day to spend more time with him, I urge you: please do it!

In spite of how busy your life may have become, perhaps due to other children or a job, sharing a game and just sitting down to a meal together to have some quiet time will play important roles in his developing a sense of place in the family and—when the time comes, as a brand new student—the self-esteem and confidence he will very much be needing.

If ever he will require your love, training and guidance, it will be when he hears that distant school bell ringing in his ears.

Ahh-tishu!

Coughs, colds and runny noses

If there's not a proverb about runny noses, I suggest there should be. Well do I remember occasions as an infant teacher when at least half of the youngsters in my class gazed up at me, noses glistening, while croaky coughs and sneezes riddled the air with infection. So regularly do the sniffles feature in a child's first year of school, rather than treat them as inevitable, parents could vastly assist their curtailment by better educating their children.

If more kids were taught best practice when besieged by coughs and colds, schools could arrest the contagious little critters in their grubby tracks, and a teacher's day would be greatly enhanced.

What do I mean by 'best practice'?

The best personal hygiene possible within the home and school. Cold and flu viruses ride on droplets showered into the air, of course, when people cough and sneeze, and spread when contaminated surfaces are touched. It's all good common sense, and the key to dampening their effects in schools and kindergartens lies squarely in awareness and good training.

But—I have an idea!

To give it a headline, it goes something like this:

KIDS AND PARENTS OF THE WORLD UNITE!
BEAT THE RUNNY NOSE
IN THE COMMON COLD FIGHT!

MANAGEMENT RULES FOR KIDS OF THE WORLD
(Includes runny noses, sneezes and coughs)

At home:

1. Sneeze, cough or *gently* blow your nose into a clean tissue or two.
2. For sneezes and coughs, if there's no time to grab a tissue, turn away from people and cover your mouth with your inner elbow. Then mop up with a tissue.
3. Put the grubby tissue quickly into a bin.
4. Wash your germy hands *properly* with soap and send those invisible slimy germs down the sink.

Obviously the guidelines must change for school; kids in class can't follow home rules. This is where parents' cooperation will be vital to success as their youngsters step out into the world.

With prevention in mind, if your child picks up a cold, keep him home for a day or two. On the days you choose to send him, teach him to have a nose-ready, *open* tissue pack in his pocket and one for his schoolbag. (Pack a small plastic bag to receive used tissues.) Some parents may choose to add 'germ-busting', antibacterial hand wipes or gel.

Slip another tissue pack in his lunch box. During training, discuss with your child where things are best kept and rehearse the 'beat the runny nose' routine so he knows what to do. Praise him for his efforts and reward his good behaviour. Your youngster has much to absorb and learn—so take your time: be a serene parent, be a patient parent and avoid causing stress.

Whether applied at home or at school, emphasise to your child that tissues, when used—and the hands that handle them—become '*very* germy'.

'G' is for germs. *Get out of here!*
'G' is for gross
'G' is for grubby, grotty or gruesome!

Turn the lesson into a bit of fun by thinking up as many grimy 'G' words together as you can. Whatever makes a youngster think, 'Yuk!', that's what your 'G' should represent. It will help instil the notion that used tissues should be bagged or binned, *pronto*—and *hands washed or sanitised* (if using antibacterials) to send the germs packing. Tell your child, 'We respect others; it's not fair to give them your cold and make them sick.' Why not post your obnoxious G-words on my blog, *www.excitingkids.net,* and we'll put them up for the kids to view.

Remind your young scholar about hands needing to be washed *with soap* before lunch. A responsible school will see this occurs during your child's first year.

To summarise the classroom rules for kids:

At school:

1. Sneeze, cough or *gently* blow your nose into a clean tissue. That means the tissue's now *germy.* Right?

2. For sneezes and coughs, if there's no time to grab a tissue, cover your mouth with your inner elbow and turn away from people. Then mop up with a clean tissue. Be quick! *Great job!*

3. Bag any germy tissues.

4. If using germ-busters, clean your fingertips with a tiny dab of gel or use a wipe and bag it with the used tissues. Bin it if there's a bin and your teacher says it's okay. Don't save the G-wipe; it has your yukky cold germs jumping all over it!

5. At lunchtime, *before you touch food,* wash your hands *properly* with soap and send those slippery germy critters down the gurgler.

6. When school's over, put your G-bag of germy tissues and wipes straight into the classroom bin, or take it home and bin it there. Remember, *always wash your hands afterwards.*

Good hygiene and clean noses add up to confident, independent children, appreciated by teachers and accepted by their peers. Since Louis Pasteur taught us to wash our hands more than a century ago, it's been *the* only way—except for modern germ-busters in convenient little packages—of blitzing contagion. In public venues like hospitals, waiting rooms and now some supermarkets—posters and antiseptic dispensers, strategically placed, encourage adults to practise sound hygiene by cleansing their hands. Yet, it is kids at grass roots level who often miss out on this message.

It's in *everyone's* interest to arrest the cycle of germs. So unless we adults take up the fight and educate our kids, the school children of the world, it seems, will continue to suffer the blight of colds and flu for times to come.

Give it some thought. Enlist the school's cooperation to introduce *best hygienic practice* and to perhaps ensure that class bins are readily accessible and that students are encouraged to use them. Better still, raise funds to install antibacterial dispensers. Speak to other parents. Strike out for change—start a grand cause! Eradicate the runny nose and all it implies!

You can support other parents by posting your initiatives, headed 'Germ-busters', on my blog at *www.excitingkids.net.* Let's spread the good word!

I leave the challenge in your hands.

Activity

Some kids are unaware they've got a runny nose.

Don't nag. Gently remind your youngster, it's time to blow his nose and teach him how to do it properly with a tissue, bin at hand, and soap and water on the ready.

For school, if using gels or wipes, show him how to use them and check that the packs are easy for small hands to open. For a child, it's like toilet training or any other set of rules he encounters as he grows. This is how you do it: step one, step two, step three; job done. What a good boy!

Remember the importance of *practice, persever- ance* and *praise.* And public recognition works wonders. Praise him for his cleverness in front of someone else and watch his confidence soar.

Fine motor skills

M any actions rely on our manual dexterity—our *fine motor skills*—for accomplishment: the small muscle movements of our fingers, wrists and feet, as well as our lips and tongues.

When we write, we use our fine motor skills. When we form words to speak, we use them—or eat with a knife and fork or peel an orange. Painters use them to paint, sculptors to sculpt or knead clay, wine makers to pluck grapes, fashion designers to sketch, guitarists to strum, knitters to knit, kids to pick noses, and anyone with a computer to drag a mouse—the entire world, in fact—uses fine motor skills to live, work and play.

Critically, for a growing child, development of fine motor skills, which typically occurs gradually from toddler-age to 12, confers the skill to grip and manipulate objects in conjunction with eye-hand coordination. Thus it is central, along with the spoken word, to advancing the ability to communicate.

Your child's mastery of the fine motor skills associated with pre-writing *before* he starts school will be key to avoiding future anxiety and bad writing habits. That is, his ability to correctly grasp and use crayons, paint brushes then pencils, for example, as well as tools like scissors, or utensils when eating, should be chief on your list—along with dressing and toileting—in preparing your youngster for school.

Developmental play through structured learning at playgroup and kinder provide early opportunities for children to begin strengthening their fine motor skills, using materials such as simple containers with lids, Lego, play dough and sorting games—along with painting, drawing and handling scissors. These can be used just as effectively at home.

In very young children, a delay in sitting up unaided, or to walk, may predict later fine motor skill issues linked to poor eye-hand coordination. Should you observe slowness in your four-year-old to manage buttons or zips, for example, or to hold a crayon or pencil between his thumb and fingers, he may need some therapy to improve his skills. (See 'Occupational Therapy', page 14.)

During my career, I have witnessed kids' irregular writing styles due to twisted grips on pens and pencils that would make a contortionist wince. In such cases it is parents and teachers who have overlooked their duties to correct the issue at an early age. Many of these children go on to suffer subsequent frustration and panic at exam time because they lack crucial legibility and speed in their writing. Unfortunately, it's a growing problem: attention in the classroom to fine motor skills, so essential for learning, is on the decline due to overcrowded curricula.

Recognition, encouragement and rewards will continue to sustain your youngster's motivation to grow and progress. Correct grip of pencils can be mastered in no time at all, using a rubber pencil grip.

This easy-to-use tool is available from stationers. Colouring, dot-to-dot and pre-writing books will also promote his fine motor and eye-hand co-ordination.

I discuss this topic further at 'Preparing the ground for cursive script: getting a grip', page 225.

Activity

Why not turn the television off and have some fun with your child? 'Pick-up-Sticks' and 'Barrel of Monkeys' games, and activities like bead threading, drawing, cutting out and using a glue stick are entertaining and fuss-free ways to enhance his fine motor skills and cognition. (*Cognition* is the subtle mental process of gaining knowledge and understanding, and using the faculties involved— thinking, reasoning, judging, problem solving, perceiving, remembering and so on, in order to learn and interact with one's environment.)

A basic and easy home activity for developing fine motor skills is to ask your child to draw a line on paper between two lines; *do not coach him*. Progressively, you can make the two lines narrower and involve some curly twists and turns. Kids quickly become absorbed; they delight in such challenges and the rewards that ride on success.

When your child uses a pencil or scissors, make sure you praise his attempts to hold them so well.

Gross motor skills

If your child's confidence and school readiness is your primary goal, gross motor skills should be high on your list. Importantly, if he spends *more than half an hour* at a time in front of the television without active movement, you would do well to heed this advice.

From head to toe, when a child stands and balances himself, when he walks, runs, dances or plays, he is employing his gross motor skills. These activities involve whole body movements using the large muscle groups of the body.

We see gross motor skills initially at work when an infant first raises his head, dipping and swaying, but soon learns to hold his head erect. During early childhood gross motor skills increase, becoming more controlled and refined into adulthood.

The ability of your child to play physically-active games as he enters school will effectively reflect his gross motor skills. He doesn't have to excel; average is enough. Just don't let him be the last kid in a group to be picked for a team—that's when confidence takes a nose dive.

Body movements like running or jumping simply for the joy of it—or catching and bouncing balls, playing t-ball or totem tennis, which aid hand-eye co-ordination—are ways in which preschoolers develop their gross motor skills. Most kids love such activities.

Smart, thinking parents who introduce a physically-active family culture for their children know they are providing the best opportunity for their future good health. Think about friends whose families play sport. Not only do they encourage a love of exercise in their kids, significantly, as their youngsters improve their skills their confidence and self-esteem also grows by spades. And if there is a more positive, happy bonding time than when kids see their parents 'mucking about' playing ball with them, I cannot think of one.

'Quality' time is a term sometimes used by parents to impress listeners in describing special times they may spend with their children. It may also infer 'brief'. Where distractions, busy lives or broken family units interfere with dedicated child-rearing, I suspect the word, 'quality', helps assuage the guilt.

Quality time is good, but what of its duration? Quality and *quantity time* spent with your child should go hand in hand—the sharing of quiet times talking, teaching and learning or just 'being' together, as well as sharing the fun and high spiritedness. Use such times in building a mutually loving, respectful relationship with your child. Take off to a park before evening or go outside to play catch or hide-and-seek. If your child cannot have dinner at the family table due to his early bedtime, when he sits down to eat, share a small meal with him—TV off—and follow his bath with a quiet story before bed. For his personal and social well being, try to involve both parents where possible, or at least take turns to be with him.

Everyday activities that develop gross motor skills can be a boatload of family fun—and should be as routine as eating and sleeping. In summer, as mentioned, turn off TV and enjoy some fresh air in the park or have a ball game of bounce and catch in the backyard. In winter, play catch with a small soft ball inside—or enjoy some hilarity with this game of *One Pin Bowling* in the hall or a room:

Find all the small soft balls in the house you can —no cricket or golf balls—and a container to keep them in. Place a family box of tissues at the end of the hall, or thereabouts, with cushions or a pillow behind it as a ball stop. Close any nearby doors.

Take turns with, say, five or six balls to stand at the other end of the hall—closer in for the young ones—and try to hit the tissue box by bowling each ball successively down the hall. When all balls are used, the bowler collects them in the container, hands them to the next player and records the number of hits he scored on a score card. The game can be made harder by turning the tissue box on its end, or easier, using more than one box.

Many muscles are developed with this pastime— those for crouching, bending, bowling, *spinning and laughing excitedly* (as kids will) tearing down the hall to gather balls and adjust the box.

Count on it, the family will love it!

The lunch box

A healthy lunch, preferably packed in an insulated box, will be a vital part of your child's school day. Let's look at lunch boxes, per se.

Lunch box styles

If you study the Web, it can be quite confusing: there is a plethora of lunch box styles, sizes and designs. If you are in doubt, ask an experienced friend to advise you, or check with the teacher about popular styles on school Open Day before your child starts, to assist his lunchtime confidence. For my book, an *insulated, easy-to-manage* box allays concerns about perishable foods, while ensuring your child can open it. An insulated lunch box with a plastic bottle included means the bottle can be filled with water and frozen overnight. Foods like cooked meats or other perishables can be placed against the bottle when the lunch is packed next day and by lunchtime, the drink is melted while the food is kept cold. (More of that in a moment.)

Healthy food choices

Examine a government website for healthy food ideas if you are not well versed in this area. Generally address the main food groups of carbohydrates, protein and fats and see that over the week, the lunch box contains a good variety of fresh, colourful food.

Fruits and vegetables will help sustain energy throughout the day. Choose breads, wraps or pitas that contain fibre, and ensure protein foods are low in fat and safely packed. A nutritious lunch is important for a positive, happy attitude and afternoon learning.

Shun sugary foods (bars, cakes, sweets, cookies and commercial mayonnaises) and high-sugar drinks (juices, cordials, soft drinks, sports and energy drinks). Training your child to enjoy water (rather than sweetened drinks) from a young age will pay dividends in good health and avoid tooth decay. Parents—plain old water is cheap, quenching and plentiful.

Save perishable milk products and drinks for home, and *read labels* when choosing flavoured milks and yoghurts for the fridge. Many are loaded with sugar and some brands contain artificial sweeteners that aren't obvious at first glance! Unadorned yoghurts and fresh fruit run rings around the commercial sugared varieties; fruits like berries and bananas make perfect partners in a yoghurt smoothie.

Variety is the spice of life

Variety in your child's lunch box will help to inspire his interest in food and keep boredom at bay. A colourful veg combo such as carrot and capsicum sticks and blanched broccoli florets, or mini tomatoes, celery sticks and snow peas with a stick of cheese or a chilled dip will be a feast for the eyes. Add a small bunch of red or green grapes and a plum or a couple of ripe apricots and lunchtime will be seen as a treat.

Dips in small containers like low-fat hommus or guacamole, or a zesty homemade low-fat mayo (see the next Activity section) will have your child's friends begging to swap lunches.

For more diversity, cut sandwiches into triangles, squares or rectangles, and change your types of breads from wholemeal sliced, to rolls or pitas or wraps and vary the spreads from butter or margarine to avocado or blended bean and vegetables before choosing your filling: perhaps high-protein chicken, lean sliced meats, chopped egg or grated cheese with leafy greens or sliced cucumber topped with a dollop of homemade mayo—or try a finely grated combo of raw carrot, fennel and raw beetroot and a few sultanas in a small tub with a plastic fork. Avoid mini packs of dried fruit as a stand alone snack—they are *packed* with sugar!

Food safety

An eye to well-being at school means food safety, of course. Ensure good hygiene when preparing foods. Aside from the obvious washing of hands with soap, food boards for raw and cooked foods should be kept separate, scrubbed and properly dried after use. Food contamination from poorly handled uncooked chicken, for example, can cause food borne illness.

As well as using a clean special board, cooked chicken should be refrigerated within the hour or as soon as it loses its steam from cooking. Incidentally, safely cooking chicken (or pork) means checking that the juices run clear before removing from the heat.

Preparing lunches for school the night before avoids morning stress. Food such as tuna or egg sandwiches or wraps can be made up, stored in the fridge or freezer and packed in the lunch box at the last minute against the frozen water bottle or a freezer pack to keep them cold. Any such food brought home, should be discarded. Stick to the old adage, *if in doubt, throw it out!* Wash lunch boxes in hot soapy water.

Water bottles: try a routine of having two on the go; it helps avoid contamination through shortcuts. Wash them in soapy water, especially round the rim, rinse, shake them out and leave to dry in the air. A dried bottle can be filled with water and frozen, allowing a small space at the top for expansion; wrap it in paper towelling when packing it next day. Two bottles means a dry bottle is always ready for the overnight freezer.

Coach your child in food safety, and ask him to keep his lunch box away from heat and direct sunlight.

Involving your child in food choices

Your child is a precious gift. Just as you should train him to understand the boundaries within which he is free to live and play, teaching healthy food choices, early, is not only responsible, but far easier than having to correct poor choices down the track.

In the supermarket, why not engage him in the fruit and vegetable section or other aisles, by discussing different foods? Involving him in some food choices will *build his independence* and encourage a positive attitude towards lunch, once he commences school.

For example: 'Those apricots look nice and would fit in your lunch box; shall we buy some?' or simply, 'Let's find something nice for your lunch box, shall we?'

Avoid speaking of foods as 'healthy' or 'good for you'—it can have an adverse impact on some kids, especially if future class mates have 'treat' foods that you reserve for home (or so your child *claims*). Don't make an issue of whether foods are healthy or not—*simply pack good foods*. If you also set an example at the home table, the experience of wholesome natural foods—with occasional treats—will become an un-questioned, expected way of eating for your youngster.

Now for some practice fun

Once you have the lunch box, your child must learn how to manage it—another strike for independence.

Be patient as he begins and don't rush to his aid; instead, offer verbal directions and encourage him to master the processes alone. Picnics offer great opportu-nities for lunch boxes to be used, or your child playing 'school' with friends will help to give the theme a nice workout. Planning lunch box meals with you at home, or partaking one day each week leading up to school, will help to *build his confidence* (to say nothing of yours) for when he is on his own.

Start with clean hands to instil the habit for school, and involve your youngster in the lunch preparation—perhaps the day before if you plan to freeze water bottles and sandwiches or other foods. Remove it next morning for lunchtime: *Yay! It's lunch box day!*

Include all the steps, from washing hands, to settling down and opening the box, unwrapping the food or opening smaller containers. Do any foods need a plastic spoon or fork? Can he unscrew the water bottle with relative ease? Did you include a straw if that is required? Check these issues as you go and correct them before the big day arrives. Practise as often as you can. Once your child understands the processes involved—from preparation through to sitting down and eating together—allow him to take the lead. Kids love directing lunch. It will foster his confidence while developing his fine motor skills.

Eating in good time

It's important that your child chews his food well and enjoys the experience. But he should also be urged to finish lunch *in good time*—say, in 20 to 30 minutes. Although this should be sorted out at childcare or kinder, some issues persist if children are allowed to dawdle over food at home. *Teachers are grateful for kids who eat in a timely manner;* slow youngsters can disrupt the class routine when schedules must be met.

A promised family treat of a restaurant or café meal is great motivation for learning this need, and provides a more formal environment where the reason for good table manners is better understood.

Remember, you are parenting for the future. Kids have to learn to cope with routine and structure. To make the error of pandering to him because it is easier or to seek his approval will only obstruct his growth.

There's a smart way and a not-so-smart way of doing things. Encouraging your youngster's independence and the confidence to manage his environment should be your goal. It's what this book is all about!

Children love the challenge of working to a deadline, whether playing a game or eating lunch. Ensuring he doesn't scoff his food, to encourage timely eating, offer an activity he will enjoy *after* lunch, like inviting a friend over, or sharing a favourite story or game. (Remember his achievement sticker when he eats in good time.) Or perhaps award a prize for the next day before lunch, asking him to help you make the low-fat homemade mayo mentioned, page 93—fun recipe next page—or an easy low-fat hommus. (Whiz up in a food processor or blender half cans of drained and rinsed chick peas and cannellini beans with a few sprigs of parsley or coriander, a good slurp of lemon juice, a teaspoon of virgin olive oil and water to thin—for adults, add two cloves of garlic.

The popular television series, *MasterChef,* offers great visuals and inspiration for kids to learn how to prepare and cook food, although in its often free-hand use of fats and sugar, caution might be voiced to your child.

Remind him to wash his hands before starting.

Activity

Greg's Funtastic Mayo (Or use your child's name)
Makes about 12 x 20 ml (1 tablespoon) serves
NB. 1 Metric tab = 4 teas; 1 Metric cup = 250 ml/9 oz

1½ tabs (6 teas) plain flour
2 teas raw sugar
Pinch salt (less than ¼ teas)
1 egg (aided by a clean empty, plastic water bottle ☺)
1 cup water (250 ml; 9 oz)
3 tabs white wine vinegar (or another favourite)
2 teas (10 ml) extra virgin olive oil
Optional extras, or to taste: 1 teas dried tarragon *or* 2 tabs fresh, *finely* chopped parsley or coriander; *or* 2 teas tomato paste *or* grated parmesan cheese; *or* 1 teas of French-style mustard, lemon juice *or* a dash of curry powder

Ask your sous chef to measure the flour, sugar and salt into a small bowl. Demonstrate how to smartly crack the egg and empty it onto a saucer. (He can have a crack next time.) *Here's the fun bit:* take up the plastic water bottle, squeeze the sides and place its mouth carefully into the egg white next to the yolk. Release pressure to suck the yolk into the bottle. *Whoohoo!* Stir the egg white into the dry ingredients a little then ask your sous chef to shoot in the yolk. Beat the mix well with a metal spoon to remove all lumps; it should be light and creamy. *Lumps mean a lumpy mayo!* Ask your sous chef to add a dash of water from the cup to loosen the mix.

If using tarragon, measure it into your helper's palm and have him press it down and stir it with his finger to release the fragrance. If he wrinkles his nose, leave it out for now; there are other choices. If it's a goer, he can throw in the tarragon and add the remaining water and vinegar. Transfer the mix to a small non-stick saucepan. You're still at the bench—the stove is *your* domain, of course.

Tell him it's your turn now, reminding him of the hazards of a hot stove. Occupy him with a helpful chore while you bring the mixture to the boil, stirring constantly with a wooden spoon.

Show him the thickened mixture carefully at the end. For a pale pink mayo, or extra bite, add the tomato paste, parmesan or other options while the mix is warm. Finally add the olive oil and beat it well in for texture and another layer of flavour.

Serve for serve, this mayo has less than four per cent (0.7 g) of the oil content of a classic mayonnaise so it's not *haute cuisine.* But it does a nice job of keeping fat low while adding moisture and a good kick of flavour to lunch box meals. Store in a glass screw-top jar *in the fridge* with a circle of baking paper on the mayo to prevent a skin as it cools. If too thick on chilling, stir in a dash of water. Use for binding fillings together, including canned salmon or tuna, chopped egg or salad items—or as a tasty dip. It keeps for weeks.

Exciting awareness

2

Family, home and friends

Author's second note

Having employed the male gender throughout Part 1, I put a friendly case to my editor for equity in Part 2, and she agrees I have a point: the boys have had a fair run. I am therefore switching to the female gender for Part 2 and will shoulder any blame from parents of little boys.

Part 3 is anyone's guess.

Life has become so demanding, so overwhelming for many parents, they are failing to engage regularly with their children—to talk about their day perhaps, over a family meal; to coach them in good manners by teaching them not to interrupt but to take turns to speak as they exchange news and ideas; and above all, to ask their youngsters questions that require them to *think* and *respond*.

During my daily stint of exercise through a local park, I often see stay-at-home, working parents, usually mothers, chatting on benches while their preschoolers run riot on the roundabouts and swings.

I sometimes wonder how many might have stopped on the way, or consciously taken their kids for a walk solely to observe and listen to nature around them: to hear a birdcall, or watch a mother bird in spring feeding her young; to look up at the colours of trees in autumn or have fun crunching dry leaves underfoot—to talk with their youngsters about the changing seasons; to awaken them to a world that exists beyond playing and television and eating and sleeping.

I wonder this because it alarms me the number of children I see who have no awareness, for example, of the seasons or the environment in which they live—other than perhaps that they wear hats in the sun, boots in the cold, and take an umbrella when it rains. Quiz some eight-year-olds about the seasons and one would think they'd been asked to quote Hamlet. As for the environment, some kids think apples come—not from trees—but the supermarket shelf. Others draw birds with four legs! I mean six to seven-year-olds, here.

Awareness has an empowering effect on young lives: I liken the mind to a bud that slowly opens to the light to see shapes and colours and diversity and detail. It carries with it the awe of astonishment in the knowing, and inspires excitement, curiosity, exploration and discovery. It brings a consciousness of creatures and their place in the environment, and leads, in time, to a deeper appreciation of family and other human beings, their circumstances, feelings and lives. Awareness evokes thought and thoughtfulness, discernment and understanding and, in the classroom and beyond, is a prerequisite of insight, and to critical thinking, evaluation and solving problems.

Awareness also builds character. It opens doors and is the well from which has sprung the creative ideas and innovations that have markedly changed lives throughout the world.

It is a potent and wonderful thing.

So, what is your role in inspiring awareness in your child? Where might you begin?

Take your child's hand, step out and have an adventure together. Explore the world at your doorstep; stop and talk about what you see and find, and enjoy her awakening to the wonder of it all. Nurtured with care, her awareness will bring rich reward.

Your unconditional love

You will have noticed that a common theme in my discussions on getting kids ship-shape and ready for school is *giving them praise* for effort and achievement. Offering encouragement, even when they make mistakes, sends a resounding message: 'I will always love you—no matter what!' This gives children the confidence to test and practise new experiences within a secure environment, and the courage to take risks in order to learn.

We need to define the difference here between your unconditional love and how you respond to your child's *behaviour*. Clearly, if she pushes another child into a puddle or deliberately scribbles all over a wall, she should be disciplined, guided and shown that unacceptable behaviour has its consequences. Having progressed as a toddler from spells in the 'time-out chair', by age four it would be fitting to send her to her room, for between five to 10 minutes, depending on the offence—or to deny her a favourite activity.

A discussion on the importance of praise and un-conditional love can be vividly illustrated by exploring the negative end of the spectrum. Harsh criticism or belittlement can be so harmful that one ill-conceived remark can change a life; a person's very existence can revolve around a single tactless comment made years before by a parent, teacher or friend. Being compared disparagingly to a sibling is a prime example.

This happened to Susan.

Susan was an intelligent woman in her early forties who had never been able to please her perfectionist father. A stats expert in a highly-paid corporate role, this man had succeeded in undermining his daughter's confidence and sense of self-worth her entire school career, relentlessly criticising and comparing her efforts to the achievements of her slightly older brother. This, in spite of her being an A-grade student.

'After reading my school report, he would always shake his head as if I were worthless,' Susan explained to me. 'I cannot recall him ever offering even a crumb of encouragement or praise,' she said.

Her eyes welled with tears. 'I will always remember overhearing him talking one day to a close family friend. He was ecstatic about my brother passing Year 12 with high honours and being offered his uni of choice, to do Law. I was in Year 11 and had also done well—not that dad had shown any joy beyond a tight smile for the benefit of my mother.

'When the friend asked about me, dad let out a sort of laugh and dropped his voice and said, "Chalk and cheese, Paul; chalk and cheese." Then he said some-thing else that I couldn't catch and laughed again. That was more devastating to me than any lack of affection or praise he'd denied me in childhood,' Susan told me. *Not knowing what he had said.* That almost killed me!'

The demoralising treatment of Susan's father infected her entire social and later family life.

As a grown woman, she sought dependent relation-ships, actively seeking approval of others in order to feel valued. She was somewhat fragile, and suffered a debilitating skin disorder. At the time of our meeting she was struggling to deal with marital issues.

Lamentably, Susan's story portrays a not un-common phenomenon within the dynamic of family relationships. While her case may seem extreme, it serves to send a message to those busy parents who may have lost sight of the fact that having brought their children into the world, there are certain parental obligations that they have a duty to meet.

Throughout childhood, in order to blossom and grow, youngsters need to be lovingly acknowledged and encouraged so that they can step out and take risks in trying new things without fear of censure. That is how we learn. That is how we become adventurous, confident and successful, and reach our potential.

I earlier asked, in essence, what you would wish for your child's future. When you sit across from her on her twenty-fifth birthday, what do you hope to find? Most of us would be glad just to see our kids as adults, well adjusted, happy in their relationships and content with the direction of their lives.

I am sure you have similar goals for your child.

In all my experience, I have rarely met parents who did not love their children. Unconditional love is, after all, the foundation stone of parenthood. We know we love them—sometimes overwhelmingly—in spite of their naughtiness or when they wear us to the bone.

Nonetheless, where parents can come unstuck is in allowing the commotion and noise in their lives to distract them from 'actively' parenting. For some, it is in failing to identify, perhaps when stressed or angry, the difference between the child and the behaviour. Several years ago, I worked with homeless kids, counselling the youth and their parents. On the surface, the causes of family dysfunction were common: parents on the kids' backs, kids pushing parents' buttons, poor parenting and coping skills, kids just being kids, and so on. But at the root of the reasons for leaving home, in many cases, was that *the children believed their parents didn't love them*. One mother had screamed at her defiant son, 'You are beyond hope, Jordan! I can't bear to look at you; you are not my son any more!'

The parents of these kids *did* love their children.

When I pointed out that they were sending the wrong message to their offspring—that they were targeting the *children,* and not their bad behaviour—the light dawned on many faces. After further counselling, some of the kids returned home.

If you think this chapter has been written just for you, you are right. The activity opposite will guide you in creating a safe haven of empathy and encouragement for your youngster, giving her the confidence to experiment and learn, and to grow in strides.

Reminder notes on doorframes and walls around the house are always a great way to transform actions into habits. My kids are grown, but three covert little stickers around the place always jolt me into action at unexpected times when I am otherwise preoccupied in thought. My reminder simply says, 'stretch'—something I forget to do after exercise or sitting too long at the computer.

All your sign need say is, 'Praise!'

No matter how small the effort or achievement, make it a rule to praise your child as she grapples with learning new skills. If she struggles to dress herself, praise her for trying; if she has difficulty opening a container, praise her for trying; if she speaks to you nicely or tidies her toys without prompting, hug her and give her a small reward; talk about her successes in front of someone else.

But it shouldn't end there. Spontaneous affirmations of love and pride—from both parents, to *each* of their children, individually—not only builds self-esteem, but contributes to warm and trusting relationships.

'You are very special to me'; 'I love it when we (go out/have fun together)'; 'you make me happy'. And don't overlook that all-powerful motivator throughout childhood to support a youngster's self-belief: 'You can do anything if you try!'

It's important you avoid the 'buts' in your praise vocabulary. Let's say she is practising writing her alphabet (we'll get to that on page 171). If she's written a row of the letter 'a', for example, find the best ones and tell her that you really like *this one* and *that one*. 'You are doing so well, darling; I am very proud of you. I can't wait to tell grandpa.'

No matter that your instincts urge you to correct her mistakes, *don't*. If some letters look wrong, don't say, 'I like this one, *but* this one isn't right.' Make a mental note to address it next time. At the early preschooler stage, it is unproductive to find fault. Your aim is to encourage your youngster to be excited about learning and to take ownership of the learning process. The 'buts' won't do it for her. We want her to leave the table on Cloud Nine and looking forward to the next time, not dragging her tail because she feels she's failed.

Count on it: she will remember the criticism.

Assertiveness and respect

The most important people in your child's life, *right now,* are you, his parents or guardians.

Next, might be close relatives or friends, kindergarten or playgroup teachers, and other kids: siblings perhaps and playmates. Throw them in the mix and in an ideal world their combined influence on your child will be wholly desirable. That, however, is not always the case. Negative effects like dominant other adults—a well-intentioned, but interfering grandparent or an estranged controlling spouse—or some unpleasant other child along the way, make your role as a confident loving parent even more vital for your child.

Kids are perfect mimics. They will copy others' actions at the bat of an eyelid. To instil positive, assertive behaviour in your child, you—and no one else—must lead the way. And when she observes then follows your example, naturally you will wish to be the very best role model that you can: a person who displays assertiveness, awareness and understanding; someone who has a clear sense of self-worth, is dependable, empathic and who invites respect from others.

'Assertiveness' does *not* mean being aggressive or demanding; it means *confident* and *self-assured* while actively respecting another's rights to hold opinions and beliefs which you may not share—and I'm talking adults, here—not the rights of kids to believe burgers and chips every day of the week should become law.

Assertive behaviour also means claiming *your* rights to the same respectful treatment: not allowing others—especially offspring—to take advantage of you. If the clear message to your child is, 'I am a person worthy of respect,' your youngster will quickly learn to look up to you as a family leader and, all things being equal, will strive in time to mirror your qualities.

You must take the helm in your relationship, not your child. You may wish to revisit this theme, pages 53 to 55. Don't fall into the trap made by some parents who fail to be assertive with their children.

Typical of this is Kathy, whose son, Ryan, was badly behaved and manipulative. He was a master at 'pulling her strings' and she had become, through lack of confidence and poor role models in her past, an unwilling puppet. When Ryan was disobedient, Kathy only fanned the flame of rebellion, using terms that blamed him for *how he made her feel*, rather than chastising him for his actions. 'You make me so angry, Ryan,' she would cry—or, 'You make mummy so sad.' Oh dear; poor, sad mummy! A defiant child would continue to wipe his little boots all over her.

In teaching young Ryan that his behaviour was unacceptable, Kathy should have asserted, with emphasis on the 'I', '*I* am very disappointed in you, Ryan,' or '*I* am not happy with your behaviour'.

Kathy made another error by responding to Ryan when she was stressed. Once, after a strenuous and trying day, he flicked macaroni pie at her across the table. She exploded, collapsed and started to sob.

I explained to Kathy that had she instantly dismissed him to his room for disrespect—not only to her, but the food she had prepared—and, importantly, removed his right to return for dessert, she would have displayed the style of firm management that all kids should see from their parents. Instead, she had poured out her anger and frustration, holding up a perfect *negative* example of how he should behave in a similar setting. Poor Ryan. What hope did the little boy have of learning *the right way* if his mother's inappropriate behaviour was constantly on display?

Fortunately for both, Kathy began to learn that being assertive and constant was key to confronting her son's wilfulness; that being the parent in the relationship meant *she* was in charge, not Ryan. This did not come easily to her. At first, she was anxious that standing up to him would make the matter worse; that allowing his antics to continue without consequences was preferable to—what she saw as—'going into battle with him'.

Conflict is a part of life. I made Kathy see that under such conditions, conflict can be useful. It's an ideal opportunity for children to learn how disagreements with others can be constructively managed.

Kathy's experiences underpin an important lesson. If your child misbehaves, let us say she whinges to stay up later than usual, or worse, shouts her demands at you, your principal indestructible rule should be that *you require respect*—the same respect that you afford her. This should be made calmly and be patently clear.

When temperamental outbursts are treated with cool composure, it can have an observable, disarming effect. In a four-year-old, the double-take reaction of, 'Hello, what's this?' is almost visible, although she may still pout and strive to appear angry.

Give her another chance to put in her request, quietly explaining that in so doing, she must speak nicely. It will be helpful to her if you demonstrate how, and what you want her to say: 'May I please stay up a little longer, daddy?' Tell her when she addresses you in this manner, then—and only then—are you willing to listen.

It takes practice like all things worth doing, but your return on time invested will be shared by you both. She will learn assertiveness and respect through your example and guidance, and you will not only enjoy the benefits, but be proud of her behaviour towards others in the years to come.

My last word on this is *don't put it off;* start when your child is an obstreperous two-year-old.

Activity

Kids are wonderful little copy-cats!

It makes sense therefore that when your child is around, you are as upright a role model as possible so that she only has chances to mimic your positive behaviour. Assertiveness lends a good example.

Firstly, allocate special blocks of time for yourself during the week that might be called, *parent's time out*, in order to take a well-deserved break from the domestic routine. This is an effective way for a demanding preschooler to learn about assertive behaviour and—in this case, how to respect another's right for time and space. Half-an-hour won't push the issue too far.

Next, engage your youngster with toys or books in the room with you—or in her room if you prefer, as long as she doesn't think she's being punished for something—and quietly announce that you are taking *parent's time out* for half-an-hour, perhaps to read or relax as you will. This means, strictly, that you are not to be disturbed. Don't close off doors, but create an atmosphere which indicates emphatically that this is *your* time.

Assertive behaviour reflects self-respect.

This strategy of requiring your child to meet your wishes, demonstrates to her that you value yourself enough to dedicate special time to relax and enjoy a personal activity solely for yourself, without needing to be always at her beck and call. Importantly, it will help to foster in your child those qualities that you are seeking to encourage.

Learning to listen

Words! They wink and beckon and jostle for attention at the core of our existence. They smother us like bees around a honey pot; they get up our noses, in our ears and in front of our eyes. We live in the thick of them and cannot be without them: words thought, spoken, written, sung and heard—that is, words heard, *some* of the time.

When youngsters learn new words, parents are quick to teach clear enunciation. But many overlook a vital dynamic. Communication is more than word delivery. Less practised by parents is teaching their children to hear a message—*the skill of listening*. Spoken words are not communicated until they are also received—consciously heard or understood.

Failed communication is a common family feature where parents don't confirm that their children have listened when spoken to. Most of us have probably been guilty of this—except perhaps when perceiving we've been ignored. 'Did you *hear* me?' an exasperated parent will be heard to say. Good. That's confirmation!

In conscious or *active* listening the mind's synapses are popping like sparklers on a birthday cake! Words are not merely heard, but processed; meaning is extracted from the information and allowed to 'sink in'.

I cannot stress strongly enough to young parents, the importance of this skill in the classroom. Active listening is *pivotal to your child's ability to learn.*

In the early learning phase, believe it or not, your child's ability to listen and absorb basic concepts, for example, before/after, over/under, up/down, soft/hard, et cetera, lay a critical foundation.

We know a building raised on a shaky base cannot be sustained, a fact borne out by the destructive forces of nature. Similarly, without a child's strong learning base, higher more sophisticated concepts such as time, the seasons, consequences, and so on, are often little processed, or misunderstood. At best, the framework for evaluating, reasoning and deduction is fragile.

So how do we teach our preschooler this important skill of active listening? Fortunately, it is easy to foster and develop.

The ability to listen means responding to tasks which involve one or more elements. A productive first step is to ask your child to follow a simple direction then confirm she has listened by saying pleasantly, 'What did I ask you to do?'

Once grasped, make the exercise more difficult by adding more details and directions. For example: 'Can you put the blue cup on the yellow saucer, please?' Praise, once again, is essential for her efforts. In a social context, children learning to listen and speak clearly, should also be taught to respond, taking turns.

Significantly, because young children receive basic concepts through an adult's *spoken* word, those untrained to listen are disadvantaged. As discussed, early gaps that weaken foundational learning can affect more complex learning along the academic path.

What are the symptoms?

Increasingly, in my work as a psychologist and educator, parents are concerned that their children cannot concentrate; that their grades are suffering. In a class of kids, pulsing with energy and distractions, such children lose focus on the task at hand. Were they taught active listening at an early age? Parents shrug and cannot recall; I suspect, chances are, no.

A client, a grandparent, rearing her ten-year-old grandson and worried about his poor school performance, offered a brief anecdote during a consultation. Pulling up at a variety store, she asked grandson, Jamie, to jump out and buy a carton of milk. My client shook her head. 'It was so typical of Jamie's problem,' she said. 'Three minutes later, he came running back to the car to ask, "What did you want again, Gran?" '

The lad had switched off—stopped listening—the moment they had drawn up to the shop, his head spinning with the world of tempting treats he knew to be waiting inside. His grandmother's request had not even skimmed the surface of his busy young mind. Jamie's parents had undergone an acrimonious divorce when Jamie was four; he had not experienced a supportive loving home until his grandparents had gained custody. I believe the lack of care towards his early learning needs had contributed to his issues. It is no secret an inability to concentrate can lead to significant frustration and learning problems that can affect a child's potential, grades and possible success in the future years to come.

You may be thinking that it's somewhat premature to be considering your preschooler's future success. 'I'll worry about that when the time comes,' you may say. But that's like trusting a plant will thrive without nurturing! When children can't concentrate, it means threads of questions or information are lost, causing confusion, and plummeting confidence and self-respect. It leaves some kids feeling 'really dumb'.

In my book *Reach for the Sky*, for students, Grades 5-12, I pose an often unrecognised reason for exam failure—and a further symptom of children not taught the skill of active listening, early—students who fail to understand the nature of questions. I ask, how can they therefore perform the tasks expected of them? *If students do not understand the question, they cannot possibly become involved in the process of constructive thinking.*

Encouragingly, I tell parents, such children can be helped when guided and offered positive strategies. Many experience a genuine awakening, realising they can have control over their learning—that it has a purpose, and that it is not just a series of mindless questions and answers that may otherwise have floated blithely out the classroom window. Importantly, when children are shown how to engage in classroom activities through active listening, their marks improve strikingly. Many move from being C grade students to becoming A grade students.

There are other reasons, of course, that may cause a student to experience a lack of focus in the classroom.

However, having studied early childhood learning, I can safely say that active listening, taught before school-age years, offers students a sound pathway to clear thinking, discernment and the ability to weigh and assess consequences. These are vital life skills.

Activity

Show me a preschooler who doesn't like playing 'Simon Says'! This timeless game is an effective aid in developing active listening skills. Complexity can be increased by gradually adding more directions to the task such as, 'Simon says, touch your nose and jump four times.'

A conditional direction makes for even greater challenge and confirms your child is listening through a correct response. For example, 'Simon says, clap your hands and touch your knees if you're wearing white socks.'

Don't overlook that your child will swell with excitement when roles are switched. Take turns, allowing her to be 'Simon'—or Simone, in today's politically-correct world—and to control the game. It will prove a great confidence-booster.

The importance of one-on-one parenting

'Where's daddy, mummy?'
Whether it's 'where's daddy' or 'where's mummy', these are the universal questions of children whose one parent within a typical nuclear family household never seems to be around. It may be due to a job, or perhaps through shirking responsibility and leaving all child-raising to the partner.

In the previous chapter, I suggested the desirability of both parents, *where possible,* setting things aside to spend meaningful one-on-one time with their kids.

For preschoolers especially, coping with the wonder and challenges of everyday life, like new activities, new friendships, new expectations and rules—and for some, the anxiety of starting school—the love and support of both parents will have a significant impact on their levels of optimism, confidence, social skills and ultimately, their academic learning. Except within single-parent families, three sets of dynamics can exist:

- the parental dynamic (between the couple)
- the family dynamic (which may include siblings and/or grandparents or others), and
- the individual dynamic (between parent and child, *including the single parent*—or between siblings)

I often use the analogy, discussing this with parents, that the three sets of relationships can be compared to the building blocks or parts of pretty much any entity, be it a house, a truck, a lawn mower or a cupcake.

Remove one component, or leave it out altogether, and the structure becomes flawed, sometimes causing serious damage.

So it is within the context of family, where individual relationships can be overlooked or break down for one reason or another. At best, this can render the family dynamic a little shaky on its feet; at worst it can collapse like a stack of cards—and the odds are, the biggest impact will be felt by the children.

Jason's family was a classic case where an often absent and inattentive father caused serious rifts *in all three sets* of dynamics within the home—that between his parents, which rendered instability generally within the household, and that between him and his father. His father had a job that took him interstate several times a week but even when at home, he hand-balled all child-raising responsibility to Jason's mother.

'I remember as a child, sensing a sort of void in my life that others didn't seem to have,' Jason told me. 'Dad was gone a lot, yes, but even when he got back, he didn't get together with me or my brother much. When he did pay attention, it was superficial; no real connection—he never looked me in the eye, and he talked to me more like a patronising uncle.

'By age eleven, I was convinced dad didn't even like me. From time to time, he'd say, "How's school, matey, how's your homework going, matey?" I think he called me, "matey" just to kid himself he cared. Next thing I'd look up and he'd be walking away. It suddenly felt false, like a lie.'

When Jason's parents split up, Jason and his brother lived with his mother, becoming increasingly disconnected from their father and rarely seeing him. Intensifying the trauma, during the early separation, the boys' mother set out to alienate them from their father making negative comments about his character and encouraging them to take her side.

Jason's past had left a deep-seated legacy. As a young teenager in a state of eroding confidence—and not unlike Susan (page 112) who could never please her father—he strove anxiously to be liked by his teachers and peers. However, to his own dismay, he found he was becoming 'the wimp'—as he called himself—that reflected the labels his mother had pinned on him. As a result, his constant bid for friends and approval exposed him to the contempt and irritation of those from whom he had sought comfort. When he was beaten one afternoon by two class bullies, his mother took him out of the school, and the cycle began again, accompanied by severe anxiety and failing grades at his new school.

Jason came to me, a nervous young man of twenty eight. He was a heavy smoker, insecure and depressed. His visit had been prompted by the threat of losing a young woman in his life whom he was desperate to marry. Not to mince words, Jason had become the victim of childhood psychological abuse and neglect.

Compounding his father's rejection of him was his mother's controlling nature. She demeaned him, and in a bid for self-respect and independence, Jason rebelled.

His mother lashed back, accusing him of being 'worthless like his father', the ultimate humiliation which haunted him and paralysed his ability to sustain enduring relationships into his adult years.

Over time, through counselling, Jason experienced some measure of healing, finding solace in accepting that he wasn't to blame for his troubled state. He did lose the woman of his dreams, but in the years that followed, met someone new and went on to make a family of his own.

I hesitated to bring Jason's story to these pages. It is not a happy one. However, I chose to do so because it serves to hold up a vivid and disquieting picture of the harmful effects on children and their parents when fragile relationships are permitted to get out of control.

It's hard work at times, this relationships thing—it takes commitment and courage. But even in conflict, one fact can assure us of comfort: we each have control over how *we choose* to react to the events and circumstances of our lives. We have the power, as individuals, to defuse potential discord *before* it becomes a mountain that's too tough to climb.

It's as uncomplicated as a simple conversation: partner to partner, parent to child, sibling to sibling— whatever is needed. It's called one-on-one engagement. Talking. Respecting others. Strengthening the ties that bind. Looking after family relationships—and like a keen gardener seeking to raise strong plants in his garden, *devoting time to their care*. For example, make a date with your youngster and hang out for a while.

Take an hour or so together to have a good time and do it on a regular basis. Do crazy stuff; serious stuff; create memories. Like this one, perhaps, heard recently from the proud father of one of my students:

'Actually, *my dad* was the muso in the family. *He* gave me my love of the guitar; we used to practise together for hours when I was a kid. *Still* do, in fact—and now, waddiyaknow? Young Sophie's got the bug!'

Activity

At least weekly, each parent might set themselves a 'sharing time' schedule of one-on-one time with *each* of their children. Nothing elaborate. Just the kind of everyday pastimes that may cause us, like the chance remark above, to tell a friend years on, 'My *mum* taught *me* how to knit,' or 'It was my dad, in fact, who gave me my love of fossils.'

The aim is to have your child see you, not as a blur in the family line-up, but as a *person* and *parent*. It's an opportunity for true friendship and to express the encouragement and pride that you feel. Its value can be felt if you are fortunate enough to recall a happy childhood and the memorable personal times that gave seal to warm and lasting bonds with your own parents.

If that's not the case, be glad for the chance to make up for what you did not have.

Sharing a united front

During a social gathering of families several years ago, my self-restraint was sorely tested by the response of one of the fathers to his five-year-old daughter's appalling behaviour. Playing in the garden with the attending kids, the child was being rude and bossy and constantly raising her voice. Her parents seemed oblivious—until a small incident.

Their daughter, Emmie, suddenly walloped her little brother over the head for no apparent reason, except perhaps that he was standing in her way. When the boy began to cry, his mother, having witnessed the attack with the rest of us, shouted at her daughter, then turned to her husband, round-eyed. *'Ian?'*

I was astonished to see Ian give his wife a wan smile and turn back to the conversation. It was none of my business, but there was evidently more going on there than met the eye. His small son in the meantime was obviously in pain, the older sister watching from the sidelines for her parents' reaction. When her mother got up and strode towards her, Emmie ran off screaming as if she were the victim. Ian squinted at his wife's receding figure and called after her, 'Leave her, Brenda, she's only having a bit of fun.'

Brenda scooped up her son and carried him back to the table, ignoring her daughter who had turned and was standing, feet astride, chest heaving, gazing solemnly after her.

Whatever the reason or power struggle in which Ian and Brenda were engaged, they presented the perfect model of parents who lacked a united front. And unhappily, they were blind to its product who lingered watchfully at the garden's edge. To the casual observer, Emmie was simply a rude and precocious, attention-seeking child. Yes, she *was* seeking attention: to my ears, her wounded scream carried a cry of both exasperation and despair—a patent plea for guidance.

Instinctively and subconsciously, the couple's little girl was searching for her safe haven, a parent's voice that would pull her back behind the boundary to keep her checked and secure. Critically, her parents' discipline would have demonstrated to her that they held her as someone special whom they valued and loved.

Emmie's behaviour, it seemed, was a normal event and had probably existed since toddlerhood. Playing up was her way of constantly trying her parents' ever elastic boundaries—one parent saying, *no*—the other saying, *go ahead, that's okay.* In testing her limits at the party, she was demanding, *yet again,* am I secure? Do you value me? Show me my place in this family.

Families are no different to any other human group, be it a sports team, a ship's crew, a nation of peoples. It all resides in the volumes of history and psychology: an absence of good leaders and rules and their compliance leads to disorder, rebellion and conflict. Likewise, without a firm and united parental front, kids become confused—unsure of themselves and their worth within the family or a group, be it social or school.

Kids who are badly behaved, kids who 'go off the rails' are often the result of poor or careless parenting and fragile boundaries.

If you value respectful family relationships and a harmonious household, then as spouses you must work *together* with one set of family rules—not different rules for each of you. Bedtime provides a useful illustration. If your partner tells your child, 'Time for bed,' then back him up. It's not a popularity contest. And once rules have been established, *be consistent and stick to them.* As we saw with Emmie, your child will probably test you at first with the old pushing the limits trick. 'Mmm, mum said 7.30; I'll just try dad for eight o'clock.' *That* is your cue.

This leads me to the second key point of this discussion. A united front not only teaches a child obedience and respect, its benefits are far-reaching and may surprise you. The time that kids go to bed and the amount of sleep they get each night not only impacts on their physical activity and ability to learn, but their eating rituals and likely levels of health—and as some parents well know, kids who sleep badly are often badly behaved.

The Centre for Sleep in South Australia found in a study of 80 schoolchildren, those with borderline or problem behaviour were five times more likely to be poor sleepers—having problems falling or staying asleep, or not getting enough sleep. These youngsters not only experienced behavioural issues, but memory and classroom performances also took a hit.

Regarding bed times and sleep and their link to eating behaviour and health, when researchers at the University of South Australia examined the habits and activities of more than 2,000 school children, they found those who went to bed later and got up later than kids sleeping and rising earlier, had a greater tendency to snack on high-fat foods, get less exercise and to become obese.

The logic seems obvious but the study findings are sobering. Even with *the same amounts of sleep,* the youngsters who both got to bed and woke up earlier were more likely to be slimmer and fitter than their later-to-bed, later-to-rise cohorts. The early birds used up more energy! They spent nearly *half an hour longer* during the day in moderate to vigorous exercise. The researchers found that on average, the night-owls by comparison whiled away almost *fifty minutes extra* in the evening engaged online and playing computer games. Tired kids are less active kids.

And if bed times and sleep have such an impact on exercise and weight, what of learning and success in class? Take a look—alarm bells should be ringing.

In a study from Tel Aviv involving sixth-grade students, it was revealed that when denied one hour's sleep a night for three nights, their cognitive ability— scientifically tested on the Wechsler Intelligence Scale for Children—had dropped to the level of a *fourth grader.* That's two years cognitive development lost through a mere sixty minutes less sleep a night. (To revisit cognition, see the Activity box on page 81.)

Head of the University of South Australia study, Dr Carol Maher, noted that sleeping patterns 'are an ingrained part of people's lifestyles'. She believes since the importance of developing healthy sleeping habits extends into adulthood, lessons on sleep hygiene would be of great value in the classroom. It's an idea I thoroughly endorse. As a young teacher, I experienced children dozing in my class through lack of bed time discipline at home. I also identified kids who had been watching up to two hours of morning television before school. They were just as exhausted and completely 'zoned out'.

When it comes to preschoolers and morning TV, I advise parents to keep it to a minimum of about half an hour—or simply to engage their young ones with colouring books or quiet but absorbing games: even something as basic as a cardboard box house with cut-out windows and doors plus a few small plastic toys or the like will keep them alert and amused without tiring them out before starting their day.

To recap—my last words have a dual message:

1. Youngsters need a good night's sleep for optimum classroom functioning and learning. But remember the research! An *early* bed time over later has been shown to produce a more alert and active child.

2. Whether bed time is 7.00 pm or 7.30, stand united! Both parents should make it clear: *bedtime is not negotiable.* Take a leaf from the French: they believe that learning to accept 'no' from their parents is fundamental to a child's healthy development.

Activity

Prepare, say, 10 family rules—on a positive note ('keep your room tidy' not 'clean up the mess')— and let your child decorate the margins with bright drawings: smiling faces, flowers, hearts and so on. Mount it somewhere for all to see and follow.

Don't overlook the power of small rewards during the rule adjustment and acceptance period, remembering that *bribes are not rewards*. 'If you put away your toys tidily for daddy, I'll give you a treat,' (the bribe), is not the same thing as, 'When you can put your toys away tidily without being asked, you'll earn a reward,' (reward for effort). Youngsters will spot the difference in a flash.

To regain control over slack rules, first master, say, the bed hour, then go to the next challenge. Kids will prod the boundaries, but most respond well in the face of a parent's unwavering wide eye.

Notes

'Sleepy children behave badly and perform poorly.' *The Researcher, University of South Australia,* July issue, story 2 (2005).

Venn, Will. 'How a good night's sleep can start in the classroom.' *UniSA News; Health and Use of Time (HUT), University of South Australia,* November, story 8 (2012).

Sadeh, Avi, Gruber, Reut and Raviv, Amiram. 'The Effects of Sleep Restriction and Extension on School-Age Children: What a Difference an Hour Makes', *Child Development,* vol. 74, no. 2, pp. 444-455 (2003).

Nipping shyness in the bud

Consider two babies: Ruby and Nicholas.

Ruby's family is a big one—lots of cousins, aunts, uncles and grandparents who celebrate their birthdays at each other's houses on a regular basis. Ruby and her baby cousin are always the centre of attention, being nursed and cuddled and bundled from one aunt to another and thence to the grandparents as the women take their turns in the kitchen. They're a noisy clan, this lot, ever ready with any excuse to throw another party.

Nicholas also has a large extended family. They don't communicate much, but dutifully get together once a year to celebrate their matriarch's birthday. Nicholas's mother is protective, soft-voiced and flinches if any rellies suggest they might nurse the baby for a bit.

Fast forward four or five years as Ruby and Nicholas begin their journey through school. One child is eager and chatting excitedly, the other is shy and clinging for dear life to the parent's hand.

No prizes for guessing which is the shy one.

Drawing primarily on the love and support of her parents and influenced by the quality and level of stimulation in her environment, a child begins to gather confidence at a very early age; being held, engaging in eye contact and vocalising with people other than her parents, are good examples of this.

The acquiring of confidence in social situations, however, demands constant nurturing—that is, regular opportunities for a young child to learn the norms of social interaction: how to relate and respond to both adults and peers. Remembering that small children learn much of their behaviour through mimicry, the manner in which you and your partner conduct your relationships and the attitudes you adopt to daily situations will send clear signals to an observing child. It makes for sound logic therefore that you practise only the behaviours that you hope to instil in your youngster. More than once as an infant teacher I had cause to draw a new child aside to quietly address the inappropriateness of certain manners or the expression of an albeit, often innocent, expletive.

Your love and encouragement aside, as your little one steps out to confront and test her environment with you, along with everyday events like shopping, taking walks, discovering nature, choosing books, and so on, making room for meeting people in groups will provide her with exciting social opportunities for play, sharing and, importantly, communicating with others.

Perhaps you are introducing your child to a new play group or kindergarten at age three or four. If she has already participated in different settings among family and friends—even brief encounters with check-out supermarket staff can be a small but significant step—she will likely slip more readily into larger groups of noisy kids, teachers and hovering parents.

Exposure to vibrant social events or gatherings at the earliest possible age will not only build *your youngster's* confidence in her formative years, but in observing her growing awareness and ability as you journey together as parent and child, your private concerns about her independence and coping skills will also be allayed. Over-protected children without such experiences are often withdrawn and vulnerable.

Should your child be less inclined at first to socialise with other youngsters, you might find the guidelines in Cheri J. Meiners' book, *'Join in and Play (Learning to Get Along)'* helpful, and it may lead you to others in the series or other titles. Find it on Amazon Books.

Activity

Small steps started early, is the rule of thumb for building social skills and confidence. Assuming that your child has already been involved in group events with family or friends, as you enter new and unfamiliar social surroundings, if she is not forthcoming, show her the way by engaging in polite talk with other adults. Then encourage her to initiate a few words with another visitor as she holds your hand—perhaps another child or parent—and next time to take a small risk, such as approach a new friend, or enter a noisy room just ahead of you. Offer her prompts such as, 'Why not ask Susie if she'd like to come over later and play?'

Be aware that *your body language* will speak loudest of all. Ensure you are stress-free and feeling happy and relaxed, and use warm and reassuring words as you are getting ready to leave home. This will tell her that she is about to enter a safe, fun and enjoyable world.

Contact with others in appropriate settings that invites excitement, curiosity, conversation, playing, and sharing with other kids, will provide most of the normal elements for aiding a youngster's social development in preparation for school. Add to that, learning to make small decisions, your offering of praise as outlined in the chapter on that topic (specifically, page 40), and a dose or two of daily hugs from both parents, and the notion of having to manage a shy or anxious child will likely never present itself.

Hovering helicopters!
Over-anxious parents

The syndrome of so-called 'helicopter parenting' has grown in recent years as anxious parents increasingly hover over their kids. Eager to protect and do their best for them, many parents make their children the sole purpose of their being, intervening as their conduit to the environment. They speak for them, jump in to defend them, obstruct their inter-actions with others, quickly correct their youngsters' mistakes and just as fast, offer answers. Some parents of one-child families can be guilty of this, habitually placing their kids under a spotlight, mollycoddling them and lavishing them with undue praise.

Such dominating parental behaviour is fraught with potential issues. Many Western kids are egocentric as it is, believing the world revolves only around them. Worried parents then fan the flames by feeding their young egos and making them the centre of all attention. When this happens—as we discussed in our chapter on praise—there is a danger a child will develop an over-inflated sense of self-importance. And conversely, there are other dangers: in an environment that does not provide normal avenues for developing new skills and confidence, youngsters can suffer severe anxiety and/or shyness. In each of these cases, they are rendered powerless and ill-equipped to respond to the everyday situations in which they find themselves.

A recent media report highlighted several jaw-dropping examples of over-parenting. Among them, ten-year-olds at school camp, so cosseted at home that they couldn't dress themselves—and another of a teenager whose mother sent him to parties with a special plate of food because he was a fussy eater!

You might have noticed helicopter parents chauffeuring their kids to school and blocking side streets when they should be letting their youngsters walk or catch a bus! You may be thinking, yes, but what about all the child abductions I see in the media? Well, let's look at that. The fact is, the world's safer now, than when you were a child: walking to school is 40 times *safer* than being driven and, in the US, the National Center for Missing and Exploited Children suggests that the likelihood of losing a child to a predator is 0.00007 per cent—in other words, for this to occur, a child would have to be left outside alone for three quarters of a million years (or, for a period of some 30,000 generations). US author, Lenore Skenazy's now highly publicised work and book, *Free-Range Kids: How to Raise Safe, Self-Reliant Children (Without Going Nuts with Worry)*, may bring you added comfort. Her website can be found at freerangekids.com.

I urge you to modify your behaviour on all counts if you think you are over-parenting. Let go a little. Allow your child to take risks and to develop confidence—to reach the normal milestones of childhood development without your crowding and stifling her ability to grow. *Give her room to be herself!*

Kids are entitled to be kids—to make mud pies, jump in puddles, be silly and laugh. They need the freedom to define independently who they are without parental interference. They need time to flex their muscles a little; explore their capabilities, make a few decisions and cultivate their personalities.

School is a significant new frontier in any child's life. Without opportunities to make errors and to deal with consequences before heading there, youngsters will not have learned resilience and the vital coping mechanisms required for life beyond the nest.

So if you're a helicopter, move away and land your surveillance craft where you can monitor your child—using common sense to keep her safe—but without your eagle eye constantly on her. I have seen it often in my practice and would warn: over-parenting can have unwelcome consequences: it may lead to your child rejecting you in later years.

Activity

Start, by moderating your involvement in your child's activities and extend her the opportunity to make small decisions, as discussed on page 18. That is, ask whether she would like to do this activity or that one; whether she wants to do it now or later. Ensure each option provides a positive outcome. For example, if it looks like rain before your walk, don't ask, 'Do you think we should take an umbrella?' but, 'Which umbrella should we take?'

Whichever she chooses, follow up her decision with an affirming comment. 'What a good choice; look, it matches your jacket!'

Allow opportunities for her to make small responsible decisions then talk about 'how grown-up she was today,' in front of others. This will help reinforce the idea that your expectations require her to be thoughtful and sensible in her choices.

When it comes to her *personality,* it is timely to mention that human personality forms during the first two years of life. If you smother your child by being over-protective or intervening on her behalf when she is learning to engage with other children or adults, well-meaning as you are, you will be interfering with her natural growth and her ability to make assessments of people and her surroundings. In so doing, you will be repressing her essential right to build resilience and character in a variety of settings and to develop individuality and personality, through *her own* experiences.

And a brief note to keep in mind for the school years: a youngster should be allowed to sort out her problems or disagreements with her peers on her own, *at school.* Don't intrude. If she does something wrong at kinder or school, hold back and let her live with the consequences of her actions.

Be aware, too much attention can be as damaging as too little. Judging *the right balance* is the key.

All in the head

Prep at the home launching pad

Author's third note

B ack to the boys for the home run—with the girls having last say in the checklist.

You may recall Alexander from our earlier chapter on praise (page 35), overly doted upon by his relatives as a gifted child, the 'validation' of which—according to his mother—was his ability to recite the capital cities of the world.

In noting this example and its negative impacts, most will probably agree that far more important for the happiness and readiness of youngsters starting school is that they enter the classroom with enquiring minds and an eagerness to learn. But that is not to say there is no need for any basic skills at all.

Preparing the ground for the academic side of school should be a natural, unhurried process perhaps through a neighbourhood playgroup, kindergarten or learning at home with a parent. There are no rules, although playgroups and kinder also offer a range of opportunities for learning to share and socialise with other children and to begin forming relationships outside of family. I recommend this, where possible.

With the following bag of skills under his belt, you can be assured that your preschooler will step to his new table on that very special day, excited, confident and fittingly prepared to begin his formal education.

Learning home contact details

It makes good sense if children learn a few simple home details before they begin school. It not only offers parents greater peace of mind in a variety of situations, but reflects their caring, and their child's sense of self-reliance and independence.

During my teaching career, frankly it both surprised and concerned me, the number of parents who had failed to teach their youngsters—even as advanced as Grade 3—their home telephone numbers and other personal contact details.

At the very least, I would urge that you teach your child the following information:

▸ child's full name and age
▸ parents' first names and surnames
▸ home address and phone number
▸ parents' occupations
▸ your region's emergency phone number

Practicalities aside, when children learn these details, it can bring home a sudden awareness of their own growth and of new beginnings, and an emergence of a responsibility not felt before. Imparted over time in an easy and pleasant manner—with a dose of fun and small rewards—these fundamental steps to independence will also contribute greatly to the confidence and character-building you are seeking for your child.

Activity

About two months ahead, in a relaxed atmosphere and giving praise for effort and achievement, teach one feature at-a-time of your child's home details. Don't rush, and have fun with him. If he struggles, ignore the issue for a few days then start afresh with a different detail, returning to the other one later.

When teaching a phone number, write it down clearly for his sight-memory, if necessary breaking it into two or three components for easier learning. My young students once came up with the idea that the first three digits of their phone numbers symbolized the number of children in the family, and the following four digits were the ages of the parents. This meant all numbers represented hundreds of kids in each family, but they had the most fun visualising the ages of some parents, all of whom were actually about thirty-something: examples like a twenty-five-year-old mother married to a ninety-eight-year-old father caused a lot of giggling and finger-pointing. The technique worked a treat, and any child who hadn't known his number previously, committed it to memory very quickly. It's a means to an end that you may not require. Kids are generally fast learners.

Once he knows his name and address, move on to the next point. Practice and *revision* will assure he can readily recall any part of the information— not regularly required—at any given future time.

Understanding the alphabet

The defining word in our chapter title is *understanding.*

Many parents believe, quite rightly, that teaching their youngster the alphabet will assist in their early days of school. Learning by rote, however, only does a fraction of the job. If he is given examples early as he learns, your preschooler will come to understand, as did we all, that the English language—and particularly the pronunciation of words—is fraught with confusing inconsistencies.

You may already be taking your direction from preschoolers' television, so a word of caution. Whilst of value, some programs may not feature the nuances of pronunciation, introducing kids instead to the *names* of letters, for example, 'a-b-c', spoken as 'ay-bee-cee', but going no further.

You can do better—and your child will greatly benefit. By showing him that each letter has a name *and* a sound, and that some have a *variety of sounds*—the 'a' in *at, acorn,* and *all,* for example, and in *aim, air* and *aeroplane*—from the outset, you can provide a platform of understanding which prepares him to expect these inconsistencies on a subconscious level when encountering new words and building his language at school.

But let us not overcomplicate the process.

You didn't need a PhD to teach your infant his first words. Don't be overly concerned, therefore, about the rules that govern phonics—*the teaching of reading based on sounds* or *the science of the spoken word*—the aim is simply to make your preschooler aware that many letters of the alphabet can make a *variety* of sounds.

Activity

The 'Letter of the Week' game

Several months prior to school, or before, dedicate one week at a time to featuring one or two different letters of the alphabet. Ask your child to start the game by selecting one 'Letter of the Week' then take it in turns to choose one or two each week, dealing with one at a time.

Once a letter is decided, both of you can be on watch to find words which begin with that letter in your home surroundings and elsewhere—for example, in story books, magazines, shops, or on billboards or other signs. Record your list of words in an exercise book so that they can be reviewed down the track.

Importantly, as new words are identified and listed, observe together that the 'Letter of the Week', which commences one word, *may* have a different sound when it starts another word.

That's all you need do at this early stage of your child's development: simply emphasise the *different* sounds—not the influence of other letters next to them. That will come in time. Remember, your child is just at the crawling stage of his long journey to becoming an independent speller.

Let's say, 'a' is the Letter of the Week'. During a shopping trip, you may buy *apples, apricots* and *art* supplies, tread on an *acorn* and bump into an *auntie*. You will note that in those words alone, there are the short and long vowels of 'a' and 'ay', plus the 'ah' sound in *art* and *auntie*.

If 'e' were the letter, you might be reading a story about an Easter bunny with long *ears* and brown *eyes* who delivers *eight* chocolate *Easter eggs*. Well, you see my point. Here, 'e' makes no less than four different sounds.

So, sound the words out to stress those differences, but leave it at that; to go into the various effects of putting vowels together or the impact of 'e' at the end of a word is too advanced and will only confuse him. However, by helping him to see that there is more than one way to use letters and sounds, you will be laying that foundation to strengthen his readiness to come to grips with it all once he starts school. The key lies in *helping him to develop an open mind.*

When the time comes, he will be ready to accept the inherent variations of the English language: for example, that although one adds an 's' to 'house' to make *houses,* the word 'mouse' does not follow the same convention, but becomes *mice;* or that 'photo', although sounding like 'foto', is not spelt the way it sounds phonetically, any more than do 'laugh', 'rough', 'cough', and so on. Such early awareness curbs a reliance on phonics, a valuable tool for *first stage* learning, but which fails to stand up in the broader context.

Remember that most kids love playing with words and you and your youngster can find a great deal of pleasure using the exercise book to write a story together, featuring, say, a character whose name starts with the week's special letter: Andy Ant, Bernie Bear, Freddy Frog and so on. Ask your child to dictate the story to you, then have him draw and colour a picture about it. Or, type it onto a sheet which can be pasted into a scrapbook, put on the fridge or pinned to a corkboard for all to see.

Read to your child often—every day, if possible. Allow him to 'read' to you if he wishes, and don't worry about him getting words wrong; to him, it's a wonderful new world, a fun part of growing up and learning to communicate.

Again, at the home launching pad, your aim is to make your child aware that:

▶ many letters of the alphabet have *different* sounds.

As he progresses at school, he will come to realise that:

▶ the greater purpose is the time-old skill of communication. In simple terms: to inform, to tell interesting stories, to express feelings or actions and events, and through reading or listening, to be entertained or to learn from others.

Graduating to 'reading' favourite books

There is perhaps little to compare with the intimacy of sharing a book with a young child.

Beginning in infancy, the familiar voice of a parent is reassuring to a child, and as he grows in toddlerhood, the mere suggestion of 'story time' can evoke excited activity and the clamouring for favourite chairs—especially where beloved tales are concerned. For many, it is a special bonding time from which both parent and child draw deep pleasure and comfort.

By about age three, if a child is read to regularly, a new awareness, separate from the story's magic or entertainment, starts to filter into his subconscious. He begins to realise that the words are not simply sprinkled on pages like freckles or the stars, but that they are grouped in lines and paragraphs in an ordered manner. He will probably perceive at this stage that the sentences flow from top to bottom and are read from left to right. As he explores the 'how to' of reading, favourite books read to him often, may also spark moments of awe where he jumps in with popular phrases like 'the fairy godmother' or 'the big bad wolf'. These are the seeds from which germinate his 'reading' passages himself—although in reality, of course, most kids simply recite what they've picked up from a story's retelling. You're on track if this happens in your house.

Despite this obvious transitional phase, some parents despair, telling me that their child is 'cheating' by only pretending to read. This is an over-reaction. It is a part of learning that kids should practise the repetition and rhythm of written language just as they parroted the spoken word from the highchair when learning to talk. It is this exploration that leads to mastery and is pivotal to early-stage independent reading.

Essentially, his 'reading' to you will offer your youngster opportunities to develop an understanding of the relationship between the written and spoken word as well as left to right eye movement and the sequential development of stories. Most importantly, by your providing wonderful tales in a positive home atmosphere you will be instilling in your preschooler *a love of books*. If you are an avid reader yourself, you will know the inspiration and deep satisfaction that this pastime can bring—to say nothing of the power and influence of books having changed the course of history and lives.

But at three or four, let's keep it simple: reading should be fun, not a chore. So fill your home with books for adults and the young alike and in your free time, try turning off the television and reaching for the bookshelf or your e-reader before putting up your feet. The pleasure you discover may surprise you—while setting an example is a peaceful and clever means to encourage the same behaviour in your offspring.

Creating his story from beginning to end is next, so after the Activity box, we'll unpack the salient points.

Once your child matures to the point of interjecting wide-eyed with questions or comments about the events in the stories you read to him— and particularly when he starts repeating favourite words and phrases as he looks over your arm, it is a good time to suggest that the 'reading' be shared. During his bedtime story, take it in turns to be the reader: you, one night, him, the next.

An effective idea is to begin with books that contain pictures only, and ask your youngster to describe the setting and to explain the story. This will doubtless unleash his highly-charged imagination but will also unconsciously assist his practice of the reading norms. Such a strategy is valuable in igniting a child's creativity as he learns to unravel the mystery of words and their stories.

After pictorial books, and in conjunction with playing 'Letter of the Week', introduce basic easy-to-read books with pictures—perhaps with one to five or six lines on a page—and share the reading, as discussed. If you spot the week's letter beginning a word, identify it: 'Oh, look! What's that letter?', then move on. Don't be concerned, as I said, about his getting words wrong; the story telling, using his imagination while exposing him to the conventions of reading, is what's important.

The school classroom will take care of the rest and your child will be well prepared.

Incidentally, if your youngster comes up with a bit of nonsense about a purple mouse or a five-legged dog, it's perfectly okay to laugh and have fun with it. Here is an ideal opportunity to praise him for using his imagination in achieving such an awesome tale. It's also on the cards, by the way—he'll probably become a scientist or a writer!

Making a story with picture cards

Grasping that all good stories, like houses, have elements built in a certain order will enable your youngster to comprehend narratives and develop his own stories. It's a lesson often overlooked. If you're prepared to immerse yourself in what can become hilarious fun and games—and I hope you are—your aim here will be to coach your preschooler about this basic story structure and sequencing of events. This can be readily achieved using a series of picture cards. (Already, I hear the echoes of family room laughter!)

You'll be amazed at the wealth of learning aids at educational shops, if you've not already found them. There are a variety of picture card games where kids can organise cards in sequence to make up a story. For example, really young children may have to work out whether a puppy is taken for a walk when the owner comes home, or when he leaves for work. Online, there's material for all ages. For young beginners, you might check out *education.com/worksheets* which, in their words, allows your young learner to spin a story and build storytelling confidence and speaking skills by selecting a card to add a new element to a story— or, *Tell Tale Card Games* by Blue Orange, on Amazon.com, for ages five to adults. Sixty cards will have your child inventing stories from 120 images of characters, emotions and settings which come neatly packed in a tin canister for up to eight players.

The fun arrives when you scramble cards to mix up stories. At the same time, such valuable play and experimentation will teach your child a story's conventions: that it has a beginning, middle and end—and as he matures, its finer elements; that there is/are:

> ▶ main and (usually) secondary characters
> ▶ a plot (no matter how simple the story)
> ▶ a challenge/problem and order of events
> ▶ a climax and resolution

In other words, the main characters have a problem to overcome, are usually challenged by adversity which precedes a climax, resolution and—for kids' stories, at least—a happy ending. Think, the old classics: *Little Red Riding Hood, The Three Little Pigs, Cinderella,* and so on.

Being even remotely aware that stories have a beginning, middle and end will boost a three-year-old's readiness to tackle more advanced story creation as he grows—and here, once more, picture cards for four- or five-year-old preschoolers, treated as a light-hearted family game, will remarkably aid the process.

Our next step is to assist our young mastermind in writing stories. Well . . . not actually 'writing' as we shall see.

If you want to add to an online collection, why not make your own picture cards? There are no reasons why you can't use a nursery rhyme, for instance. Suggest to your youngster that he plays the teacher and you, the student. This gives you the chance to scramble the cards in the wrong order. Once it's unravelled step by step, your child will begin to see how a story's *sequence* of events is essential for the story to make sense.

And don't forget—praise him for his efforts!

The joy of 'writing' a first story

'Grandma, grandpa, come in—come and see! Mummy and I have written our own story!'

That's the level of enthusiasm you would hope for when your preschooler discovers the 'writing' phase of his learning curve. But as in the 'reading' transitional period, at four, a child may convince himself he really can write words even though a parent may role play as personal assistant, typing or writing out his dictated adventures. Encourage and applaud this! *The more that kids write, the better they read—and the more they read, the better they write.* That is my experience with thousands of students over the years.

From their very first week of school, pencils and crayons a flurry, I had youngsters spilling breathless stories onto paper in a kaleidoscope of colours on a multitude of topics. That they didn't all know their alphabet or how to spell their words was not my concern. It was what was going on in their young heads that I was keen to see—did they have the cognitive skills to devise and develop a storyline and transcribe their thoughts onto paper? Indeed, as the first sparks of creativity soared to the ceiling and collided in the air, who would have dared to hold up a stop sign to question the spelling? At the risk of repetition, preparing for school should be *fun* for a child—every activity positive, each outcome successful.

Young kids love 'writing' about pretty well anything.

They tend to progress in leaps and bounds, particularly, when encouraged to listen to a story then write their own version. They love to make a story their own! After sharing *Goldilocks and The Three Bears,* for example, try asking your child to create and write *his* version entitled, *Goldilocks and The Three Little Pigs!*

This chapter's discussion has promoted the general fun idea of writing to your child—the 'let's pretend' of writing, just as he might play at being a grown up.

The suggestions in our next chapter will move him towards identifying letters and words in a more concrete manner, advancing to the true starting block of being writing-ready, not merely 'writing'. For you as a parent, the difference will flag a thrilling milestone in your child's development and exciting times for your aspiring young student.

Activity

If you have a colour printer on the home front, it's relatively easy to convert your child's imaginings into colourful and exciting professional stories. You could also scatter a small handful of words linked to your 'Letter of the Week' throughout the text, although I would caution their overuse in case they detract from the delight your child takes in owning the project. And keep in mind, kids *love* to see their stories fixed to corkboards or fridges for the family to admire.

A simple story idea is to take a moment like finding a caterpillar in the garden and having your child create Caterpillar's Adventures, dictated by him and illustrated once you have typed the story.

Risk-taking is a recognised predictor of success. If your youngster can hold a pencil or pen and make one or two letters or more, encourage him to 'write' the story on his own as a first draft, ensuring he has the freedom, be it the case, to make scrambled eggs of his project if necessary.

It's easy! When he's done, simply suggest he read his story aloud while you type it. Highlight the positives and—should he be up to stringing letters together—ignore 'words' spelled incorrectly. In fact, don't correct a thing! Why pour cold water on his great little effort when he thinks he's created a masterpiece?

These stories, made into little books, often become treasured mementos of a happy childhood. But their value far exceeds a warm memory. The joy of discovery and learning, and the rewards of accomplishment are the lessons reaped from such early pastimes. In turn, they strengthen a youngster's motivation and confidence for active reading and writing during his school years.

Such skills open the doors of opportunity and endure for a lifetime.

Let's find a word starting with . . .'b'!

Inspiring a regard for others in kids and putting them in touch with their surroundings was a topic discussed in our section on 'awareness', page 105. This awakening to the world can have a lasting effect on their curiosity and eagerness to learn—and it plays no lesser role when they are learning to read and write.

Ever had a pink or yellow car, for example, that you thought was a relatively rare item? The minute you got on the road, suddenly you were aware of pink or yellow cars at every turn! It's the same for youngsters when they begin to realise that learning to read or write is a power within their grasp. Once they start looking for specific letters—say, during 'Letter of the Week'—they find them everywhere. Try getting them to stop! *Hey, these letters are speaking to me; they make words!* Next, they're searching for whole words in their storybooks. Out of the blue, that mindless jumble of yesterday's hieroglyphics takes on epic dimensions of discovery.

This new awareness becomes a spur to find meaning in words—and it is here that the foundations are laid for the more complex critical thinking and analysis of a student's later years. 'Finding meaning' is the common thread. Learning to read or write, when this first happens, the sense of excitement and empowerment can be overwhelming in kids. It's a special moment. I would love to hear of *your* child's response. My contact details can be found on page 239.

So—in your child's quest for meaning, let's offer him a treasure hunt, actively searching for the *most frequently used words* in his favourite story book. The Activity box below has the drill. After that, if this is your first child, there are details on how to locate or make a simple but entertaining card game to enhance his memory and word recognition. It's a great little activity to aid his progress once he begins school.

Activity

We'll come to our card game in a moment.

In the meantime, lists of the top one hundred *most frequently used words* can be found on the Internet, but frankly, we don't really need them. Since there are often-repeated common words in story books for youngsters, it's just as easy to make a 'do it yourself' list. Take up a favourite story and ask your child to trace his finger through the sentences to find a word that regularly occurs. If he identifies 'a' or 'to', for example, explain what it is, have him write it, and then search for the same word, recording the number of times it occurs on a page.

Don't rush this process; let him absorb the words at his own pace; he may even let you know when he's ready to find more words over the next day or several days; it differs with each child.

Another approach is to start by suggesting your child finds, say, short pronouns, one at a time: 'I', 'he', 'it', 'we', etc, or prepositions: 'on', 'at', 'in', 'by' and so on. Once mastered, have him advance to finding slightly longer words: 'and', 'was', 'the', 'but' and 'then', for example.

You could also ask him to locate key words relevant to a story's meaning. For example, the word 'train' in *The Little Engine That Could* and then a whole term like 'Little Blue Engine'—or the word 'hood' or whole term 'Little Red Riding Hood' in the classic of the same name.

Keep the list of words and terms you cover to allow for easy revision, perhaps giving a small reward for success such as an extra story at bedtime simply for his listening delight.

As your youngster builds his repertoire of words, an effective extension is to search for words that begin with specific letters—'Let's find a word starting with . . ."b!" '—so that as all the 'b' words are found and spoken aloud, your child can see what they look like in written form. Youngsters more quickly grasp the relationship between the spoken and written word with this technique.

A wide range of 'learning to read and write' tools is available for preschoolers in stores and online. Try *Leap Frog* at www.leapfrog.com.

Now to our card game, *Concentration,* or *Memory,* where the aim is for players—you and your child, or he could play solo—to match pairs of identical words from two sets of cards, each word printed on a down-turned card. You may know it by another name.

Online, turn-the-card-and-make-a-match games like 'Sight Words' can also be played freely at www.primarygames.com/langarts/sightwords or by subscribing at www.education.com at a small cost to download a variety of matching word or picture -card memory games as well as printable work books. However, if you take a look there, you might be inspired to make your own 'matching word' game. Use paper if you wish but a sheet of light card would be more practical; print the words freehand or on computer.

Don't overwhelm your youngster with too many cards when you play the game the first time. For beginners, use say, four easy words like 'a', 'to', 'I' and 'am' to start off, with each word printed on two cards. Clarify meanings where necessary.

Mark one set of cards on the opposite side with red dots, the other set with blue dots. Place the cards, words-down, in an arrangement of two lines of four, alternating each colour—red card, blue card, and so on—and you're ready to begin. Players take turns to flip over a card from each set.

If there's no word match, the cards are turned down again for the opponent to have a turn. Naturally, a point is scored for each pair matched.

Memorising each word's location and matching them successfully is a stimulating exercise for preschoolers, which can begin using matching pictures, rather than words, from age two or three. You will find this simple fun pastime a great tool in your youngster's mission to read and write, and importantly for his future learning. It will extend and strengthen his 'working memory' and impact appreciably the brain's ability to hold and process information.

It should therefore come as no surprise that *working memory* is a cornerstone of learning.

The ups and downs of over and under:
basic concepts and following directions

N ot all kids follow directions easily.

When it comes to grasping basic instructions involving concepts such as *up, down, over, under, above* and *between*, as a psychologist and educator I see an increasing number of youngsters who struggle. Despite normal intelligence, for a small number of children it may imply auditory processing concerns or difficulty comprehending verbal language, issues that are managed by specialist practitioners.

However, it surprises and concerns me that both schools and parents are failing to ensure that children in general are being taught *basic concepts* as a normal part of their developing vocabulary. Importantly, in their absence, the subtleties of an instruction can be perplexing to a child.

To illustrate—directing him to place his hand *above* his head, is not the same as placing his hand *on* his head. More sophisticated notions, moreover, can put a child under unnecessary stress. He may cope with a request to 'stand *between* the chairs', but be totally confused by a slightly more complex instruction to 'place two blocks *between* two rods'.

Critically, if missed and not corrected, these deficits can affect a child's learning potential as he grows, and may have a marked impact in turn on his confidence and sense of self-worth, well into childhood.

A preschooler's brain develops at a great pace; faster than at any other future time. During this growth period, a child's early experiences shape his brain's architecture—in other words, its structure and neural connections—and in a positive environment, facilitate language development and learning. Remarkably, these events from birth to kinder-age lay the foundations for all the cognitive skills that kids need in life. I think it may safely be agreed, *every day is a learning day* for a preschooler.

Grasping basic concepts are a part of this, and a clever parent will infuse them seamlessly into a child's domain during games, daily chit-chat, reading books, and so on. Illustrated story books, particularly, will prove a useful source of revision. For example, let's consider the basic concepts 'inside' and 'outside' from our list, page 212. You might point to a picture of a girl looking out the window at a rabbit in the garden, and ask your youngster, 'Is Jane *inside* or *outside* the house?' When that is established, you would ask, 'And where is the rabbit?' If the answer is 'outside'—good work! It's a wrap: *inside, outside* is done and dusted.

There are many basic concepts, of course, which fall into various categories such as quantities (empty; full), emotions (happy; sad), textures (coarse; smooth), and so on. Most of them have antonyms, although shapes and colours, for instance, are exceptions. Teaching your preschooler as many as are practical *before* he goes to school is the best advice—and following, opposite, a few activities will ferry him on his way.

Enter, once again, our traditional classic game of 'Simon Says'.

'Simon Says' is tailor-made for encouraging youngsters to explore and come to grips with the basic concepts under discussion. The game was suggested in our chapter, 'Learning to listen', page 125, to develop active listening skills.

Remembering that kids love the excitement of controlling the game, once it gets started, your youngster's understanding will progress in spades when he's given the chance to play Simon. It means he must think through his directions and how they should look *before* he gives them. This is also a useful skill-building strategy for promoting his ability to predict a situation's likely outcome.

Mistakes—yours, intentional, his, innocent—will not only add to the merriment, but keep your preschooler alert to the subtleties of meaning. In *some* contexts, for example, 'below' and 'under' might be transposable, but in others, their finer shades of meaning set them apart. Take: 'She sat quietly *below* the window'—and—'She sat quietly *under* the window'. Whilst 'below', would be more explicit, both are valid descriptions. However, these words are not interchangeable when you write: 'The sun sank *below* the horizon.' The concept of 'under', here, would clearly be unacceptable.

One can see that even the brightest of small minds might be challenged when these finer nuances are transferred to 'Simon Says'. Using the same examples, take a direction to 'put your hands *below* the table'. Lowering your hands a little and holding them near, but not *under* the table, presents the perfect opportunity to demonstrate the difference between these two words. In fact, stepping away and holding them below the level of the table top will have a stronger visual impact, clearly defining 'below' not 'under'.

Conditional directions—where 'if' is inserted in a sentence—is another effective way to encourage concept understanding. We saw this on page 131, again, when testing your child's listening skills: 'Simon says, clap your hands and touch your knees if you are wearing white socks.'

Such conditional directions can also be transferred to games with youngster's toy sets by saying to your child, 'If the garage is yellow, put a red car *beside* it.' Go one further when he's ready: 'If the garage is yellow, put a red car *beside* it and a green truck *away from* it.'

And this one, for the less mechanically minded: 'If the house is blue, stand Barbie *in front* of it.'

One more for the road: 'If the house is blue, stand Barbie *in front* of it and Ken *at the back*.'

If the house is pink, ideally you shouldn't see a hair move, in which case you would give fitting praise for careful listening.

You might also congratulate yourself that your invested time is paying off—that your little preschooler is grasping a good number of basic concepts in preparation for the big day.

Most kids should have mastered an understanding of those listed in the following table at least by the time they reach school age.

Basic Concept	Opposite
above	below
always	never
around	through
before	after
beside/next to	away from
big	little
easy	hard
fast	slow
first	last
front	back
full	empty
happy	sad

Continued over/

Basic Concept	Opposite
hard	soft
heavy	light
high	low
hot	cold
in/inside	out/outside
in front of	behind
long	short
loud	soft
more	less
noisy	quiet
old	new
on	off
on top of	underneath
over	under
same	different
sharp	blunt or dull
smooth	course or rough
tall	short
thick	thin
top	bottom
up	down
young	old

Counting to 50

We live in a world governed by numbers. Even when we use the terms '*an* idea' or '*a* house', we are assigning the number *one* to a concept or object which translates to an image in our minds. In teaching our kids to count, therefore, our aim is to equip them to understand and navigate this world—to realise that knowing how to count allows us to establish or weigh the value of something or to follow directions, whether we are buying cans of soup or works of art, or a book for five dollars, or adding three eggs to a cake.

With all this happy learning going on, fruitful though it may be, the little ones have a lot on their plates. For that reason, in my view, it's neither helpful nor necessary, to coax your child to count as far as one hundred before reaching school age. He will learn quickly enough. In the long term, far more effective is to *set the groundwork* for the number-related activities that will occur all too soon in the classroom.

Kids are concrete thinkers till about age twelve. Before then they learn best, manipulating objects and using diagrams. Sighting and counting different objects—inside and outside the home—is therefore an engaging way to encourage your youngster to count—and like many learning exercises, can be turned into a stimulating game. Remember that we are seeking to build a robust healthy brain, not dull the mind with mechanical rote learning.

Recently I dropped in briefly on friends as they were preparing Sunday lunch, assisted by their four-year-old son, Robbie. Robbie was sitting up at the bench, busily counting green beans from a bag, a small frown of concentration on his face. His mother had asked him to count out twenty-four beans, so that each family member could have six each as part of their meal. When I left, young Robbie was still at it, filling a fresh order from his dad to supply him a dozen new potatoes. I remember thinking as I reached my car that growing up in such a vibrant household, Robbie would never be part of the increasing number of 10-year-olds I see who cannot explain the meaning of 'a dozen'. In offering a clue to these kids if I ask them to draw me a carton of eggs, even then—four times out of five—I meet a blank or puzzled look that has me seriously questioning whether young families still eat eggs.

Activity

Everyday activities can be turned into a counting game adventure! Here are a few ideas:

Start early at the home toy box. Have your child build a column of blocks, counting as he goes, with the height of the column dependent on his stage of learning. Next, *you* build one using one less block, and ask him to establish by counting, which column has more. Extend that then by asking, 'How many *more* blocks are in your column than mine?'

Start another conversation: if your child sends cards to relatives on special occasions, open your address book. 'Oh, look, here's *another* number— at grandma's address. It's number . . . *21!* Why can that be?' Then you explain, improvising as you go. 'There are *thirty* houses in grandma's street.' (I have no idea how many houses were in my grandma's street—or mine, now, as it happens— so you need to wing it a little, here.) Sorry, go on: 'Each house has a number at the front.'

'Why?' asks your ever-inquisitive four-year-old.

Great question! 'Well—when you send a card with number 21 on grandma's envelope, will the mailman know which letter box to put it in?'

You'll either get a slow smile of recognition or a soft little 'I don't know,' in which case you'll need to explain, using an envelope and drawings. House numbers can be reintroduced next time you both take a walk. Identify yours firstly, then stroll to the start of your street—or find a shorter street—and check out the house numbers on the way back.

To keep up the game, on shopping trips try counting cars. Ease in, looking for red ones. If it's like here, switching to silver-grey vehicles will see your budding mathematician reach fifty before you get home! But there are many things to count: men with caps, girls in blue jeans, white picket fences, fire hydrants, motor bikes, dogs on leads.

At the market, there are questions to ask: 'Shall we buy three apples or four? One for you, one for Dad, and one for me. That's how many? *Three!* And if we buy four, how many spare apples would we have? *One!* Well done!' And so it goes. Where shopping is concerned, the marketplace becomes one big colourful classroom.

These everyday activities will start to instil a new mindset in your child: an awareness that numbers have meaning and purpose that allow us to quantify objects and bring order to our world.

To reinforce this learning, why not take a lead from Robbie's parents? Encouraging a task-sharing mindset in your child especially around meal time is a clever move that can serve a dual purpose if you commission your youngster to take up a bag and bring four potatoes and three carrots from the cupboard or pantry.

You may notice, incidentally, that being engaged in this way is not a chore for your child, but major entertainment—so take my advice: profit while you can. Once he's learned to count, being the kitchen hand is bound to lose its shine!

Is 'seven' less than 'eight', or more?
Easy learning with *number lines*

There's another side of numbers we need to cover. Bedding down an understanding of the relationships *between* numbers will be important preparation for your preschooler's learning right through school. And to fully grasp these concepts, kids need hands-on experimentation and plenty of practical, concrete play.

As in-house psychologist and CEO of my tutoring organisation, I am ideally positioned to observe trends in education across hundreds of schools. In recent times, governments in the West have invested funding and applied national assessment programs towards improving student academic outcomes. Despite well-established systems now in place, in terms of numeracy, many children, nonetheless, even in *third grade,* lack real understanding of numbers and their relationships. To their detriment, in first grade, schools tend to move kids too quickly to ready-made work sheets featuring spaces for effortless answers. Expedient, yes, in a time-poor world, but true foundational learning only comes through exploration, evaluation and play in the manner we've discussed.

Parents at home with their children, can reverse this trend, using a basic technique. It's called the *number line!* It astounds me that such a great little tool—a simple line on a page—is so often ignored. Check the Activity box for more.

Activity

Kids thrive on number lines when playing 'school'. In this case, the parent's role is student—which lets you make 'mistakes' to keep your child alert and on his toes—while your youngster plays the teacher. Teacher will *love* correcting you!

This is all you do: draw a horizontal line across a page and evenly record the numbers from 0 to 30, or so. Like this, but make it wider:

---

1   2   3   4   5   6   7   8   9   10   11   12   13   14   15...

Number lines will allow your preschooler to effectively learn *relative* values of numbers because he can see their relationship along the line. Test this by asking him to find the number that is *one more* than seven. 'Oh, there we go . . . *eight!* Then say, 'Is seven less than eight, or more than eight?' *Is it a bigger number or smaller number?* To revisit our last chapter, 'If I had seven blocks and you had eight, who would have the most; you or me?'

Try another one:

'Is four smaller or bigger (less or more, lower or higher) than thirteen?' Great! Now circle any two numbers along the number line and ask which is higher.

Remember that praising him for success will pay good dividends and make him eager to learn more.

This brings us to the next phase: the development in children of an automatic response to different number 'concepts' such as, for instance, what an image of *three* looks like, or what *six* looks like. This is implanted in the mind through repeated sighting and recognition of such concepts (we'll get there in a moment) and understanding their meaning and value—much like the colour concept of a red traffic light. *Reflexively you stop!* No thought required. Your brain has been wired to cause this response. *Meaning* makes you stop (it's red); *value* lies in not getting a ticket or running down some hapless individual.

Taking the concept of 'three' as an example, what forms might you encounter in your day?

Assisting your child with number concepts can be found once again in our picture card game. You will recall we used picture cards in our chapter on creating stories (see the Activity box, page 189).

Again, prepare two set of cards, but *six* cards to a set. In bright colours, on each of four cards draw a different symbol expressing the concept 'three'. For example: three green balls or apples, a blue triangle, three pink short lines, and a big fat red '3'.

On the two remaining cards, draw an orange square and a black number '7'. The colours don't matter, just make them strong and different, to be easily seen. Repeat the same coloured symbols on the other set and mark one set of cards on the opposite side with green dots, the other set with black dots. Shuffle the sets separately and place both sets, symbols-down, in an arrangement, say, of four lines of three, and like the former game, alternating each colour—green card, black card, and so on.

This play is a little different due to the two cards in the sets that are *not* concepts of three: the square with *four* sides and the number 7.

Players take it in turns to flip over one card from each set and if there's no symbol match, such as three green balls matching three green balls, the cards are turned down again for the opponent's turn. A point is scored for each pair matched— however, should a player take a turn and flip up a wrong card first, such as the square or number 7, he must forfeit a second try. This not only enforces the need for concentration to locate a 'three concept' first—in turn, embedding *images* in the mind of 'three'—but the idea of accepting the rules of the game. You might purposefully flip up a square or number 7, to demonstrate to your youngster how to lose with dignity.

Preparing the ground for cursive script: getting a grip

I would like, here, to revisit the topic covered on page 79 of *Fine Motor Skills* to underscore one thing—and if there are carpenters or artists or builders in your family, I'm sure they'll agree: as an apprentice, how you learn to hold your tools will affect your performance and the quality of your work, in times to come.

With this in mind, I saw a student last week whose mother had warned me that her son's handwriting was abysmal. 'Stilted and messy,' were her words, and she asked whether along with developing his essay writing skills, I could help him correct it.

Josh was thirteen. The moment he took up his pen with a stranglehold grip, I saw his first problem. As he commenced writing, his style was awkward, his words ill-formed and he began many letters from the wrong end, which inhibited fluency.

Today, computer keyboards have overtaken and consumed old modes of communication. Nevertheless, day-to-day situations and particularly students at the most critical times of their lives—*exam time*—require the mastery of an essential tool: strong penmanship.

Like an artist or carpenter, in a sense your child is preparing now for his apprenticeship—his first year of school—and at this early stage, a primary tool will be his pencil or pen. I would therefore ask, 'Is he coping? Does he hold his pencil correctly?' If it's still a little wobbly, remember, old habits are much harder to fix.

It's easy to address, so I urge you to add this short-term task to your prep. In writing by hand, adults who choose to print—and I know one or two—are likely reluctant to display a poor handwriting style, and such problems often have their roots in an incorrect grip from early childhood. Printing does the job, of course, but an accomplished fluent *cursive script* is so much more efficient and from a student's viewpoint, serves them well in their academic and later years.

This was demonstrated recently by University of Washington's Professor Virginia Berninger, at an educational summit in Washington, DC, who showed in her study that primary students expressing their ideas in compositions were able to write more words, more rapidly by handwriting, compared to using a keyboard.

Interestingly, brain imaging has also revealed that the actual process of cursive learning sparks neural activity that doesn't occur with visual typing practice. This active learning process enhances both student cognition and fine motor skills—students must multitask as they practise and learn, *focussing* on how to form the letters, *visualising* the letter's relationships to one another and *commanding control* of the fingers. The research serves to highlight the extraordinary link between the brain and movements of the hand.

Science aside, you may well agree when reflecting on the older people in your life, a mature, beautifully handwritten style embodies such character, distinctive ownership and sense of a life well lived that printed forms and typing simply cannot express.

In these modern times, when youngsters first learn to write, the printed letter style prepares them for their subsequent graduation to cursive script—a mere joining of the letters they already use. No doubt, this is how you learned also.

Practice is key to kids learning the right pencil hold (stores carry rubber pencil grips)—and to developing handwriting fluency. And where better to hone their skills than pretending to be in their first classroom? Playing 'school' is tailor-made.

You may be happy noting your child's pencil hold is good and leave it at that. Once he starts school, you are right to expect that his teacher will take it from there. However, some kids are eager to do more at home, in which case your next aim should be to confirm the writing system that will be used by his school and obtain worksheets (check online) for tracing and practice. Josh's problem apart from his grip was that he stroked his letters backwards which forced him to stop and start again.

Worksheets and pencil grips are great kids' aids.

Notes

Berniger, V. 'Evidenced-Based Developmentally Appropriate Writing Skills K-5: Teaching the Orthographic Loop of Working Memory to Write Letters So Developing Writers Can Spell Words and Express Ideas.' Presented at *Handwriting in the 21st Century?: An Educational Summit,* Washington, D.C., January 23, 2012.

James, Karin H. and Atwood, Thea P. (2009). 'The role of sensorimotor learning in the perception of letter-like forms: Tracking the causes of neural specialization for letter.' *Cognitive Neuropsychology* 26 (1), 91-100.

Klemm, William R. 'What Learning Cursive Does for Your Brain: Cursive Writing Makes Kids Smarter.' *Memory Medic,* March 14, 2013. Article in Psychology Today: http://www.psychologytoday.com. (William R Klemm, D.V.M. Ph.D., is a Professor of Neuroscience at Texas A&M University.)

The ICing on the cake!

We are at the end of a brief journey, you and I. In closing, I hope this handbook will play a meaningful and useful role as you each prepare for a major event in your youngster's life: the first year of school. In returning to the chapters and the topics we have covered, you will see that from the start, the skills championed—from dressing, to the tricky sticky talents of coping with toilets and runny noses—have *independence* and *confidence* at their heart.

If I ever become a conjurer, I'll see to it that all kids everywhere are raised in a vibrant home atmosphere. Such a home will foster curiosity. It will reward good manners, a keen competitive mind, and nurture the independence a creative life demands. Its atmosphere will stir excitement. It will promote resilience and a robust spirit to meet the personal challenges that every day will bring—new experiences, change and unexpected events. And in such homes, kids will be taught the wisdom that where they lack control over *any* situation, they will always have *the power to choose how they respond.* But—enough of dreams!

This book also aims to buoy *your* confidence as you guide your youngster in the coming months—your confidence will be catching! Most of all, I urge you: in this process, reflect on your parenting; go beyond the present and *parent for the future.* Your child's success and happiness will reward you manyfold.

Unlike maths or comprehension, independence and confidence are not concrete factors measurable in a school assessment test. To the casual observer, such personal qualities may elude the first glance; indeed in a first or second grader, they may still be budding works-in-progress.

But you and your child's teacher will know.

When you therefore look back over the first school year, I hope it will be with conviction; the clear knowledge that, inspired by your coaching and love and encouragement, your son or daughter has found the right path, developing a mindset of confidence and independence to allow them to meet whatever lies ahead.

That is our ultimate goal—it's *the icing on the cake!*

Greg Nicholson, 2014

Checklist:
'Skills and Situations'

The checklist, following, will allow you to tick off the topics covered when you've completed them. Page numbers relate to the chapter or page featuring the skills and situations.

The question?

Does your child have, or is your child able to:

Page	SKILLS AND SITUATIONS	☑
23	PART 1 – Your preschooler's physical word	
49	dress and use buttons and zips?	
57	tie shoe laces?	
61	use the toilet and care for herself?	
69	cope with a cold and a runny nose?	
77	fine motor skills for pre-writing, threading beads and tracing between two lines?	
85	gross motor skills for basic games?	
89	manage her lunchbox and open a drink?	
96	eat lunch within a reasonable time of say, 20-30 minutes, and be amenable to what you offer?	
101	PART 2 – Exciting awareness	
109	parents' unconditional love and support; self-belief through positive parent affirmations?	
117	positive, non-aggressive behaviour and self-esteem through careful parent modelling of self-respect? Parents use 'I', not 'you' statements: 'I don't like your behaviour' not: 'You make me feel angry/sad.'	
125	respectful listening skills without interrupting; after listening, can she follow tasks containing one or two elements?	
133	a belief she is important to both parents, reinforced by each spending one-on-one time with her?	
141	an understanding of family rules through a *united* parent front; behave well in and out of the home?	
149	greet old and new friends with social ease. If shy, is she conquering this through exposure in social settings and copying your lead, speaking to others?	

Page	SKILLS AND SITUATIONS	☑
155	resilience and strength of character through your allowing opportunities for her to fail—not molly-coddling her and being over-protective; will she try new challenges a second or third time for success?	
161	PART 3 – All in the head	
167	recite home contact details: address/phone number?	
171	understand the relationships between letters of the alphabet and their sounds—that a letter can make *a number* of sounds?	
179	'read' her favourite books, left to right and top to bottom? (Pretending by reciting is fine for now.)	
185	arrange a sequence of picture cards to tell a story?	
191	keenness to 'write' a story, dictated to and typed or handwritten by you?	
197	find high frequency words in a story, and locate words starting with specific letters?	
205	understand key concepts, eg: over/under; in/out and follow directions that use them?	
213	count to around 50?	
219	understand relationships between numbers on a *number line*?	
225	hold a pencil/pen correctly? [Although not essential, she may have also practised tracing numbers using her future school's approved worksheets (check online for similar material) and knows the starting point of letters and numbers when scripting.]	

For Greg's contact details please go to his blog, *www.excitingkids.net*

Psychologist, educator and author, Greg Nicholson, was born in Melbourne, Australia. During his early career, he held a broad range of teaching posts, including infant teacher and school principal with the Department of Education, before graduating as a psychologist.

Greg has played key roles in a number of academic and youth welfare programs including The Sir Edward Dunlop Program of which he was Chairman, and the Ardoch Youth Foundation. He has drawn inspiration for his latest work from his love of teaching young children, his studies of early childhood learning and as CEO and in-house psychologist of his tutoring practice, Edworks®, where he oversees the annual learning of hundreds of children, and is an innovator and policy maker in supplemental education.

Contact Greg at:
www.excitingkids.net

*A single moment of understanding
can flood a whole life with meaning.*

ANONYMOUS

www.ingramcontent.com/pod-product-compliance
Lightning Source LLC
Chambersburg PA
CBHW070952040426
42443CB00007B/475